9-30-96
Food for Thought

p. 51 - Chagall
62 - Renoir
74 - double-headed snake
76 - Samuel Hearne
80 - ready to be found
101 - photograph?

Poets of Contemporary Canada
1960-1970

Edited and with an Introduction by
Eli Mandel

General Editor: Malcolm Ross

A New Canadian Library Original

M&S

© McClelland & Stewart Limited 1972

Reprinted 1994

Canadian Cataloguing in Publication Data

Main entry under title:

Poets of contemporary Canada, 1960-1970

(New Canadian library; no. 07)

ISBN 0-7710-9506-6

1. Canadian poetry (English) – 20th century.*
I. Mandel, Eli, 1922-   . II. Series.

PS8291.P65 1989   C811'.54'08   C89-094047-9
PR9195.7.P65 1989

Manufactured in Canada by Webcom Limited

McClelland & Stewart Inc.
The Canadian Publishers
481 University Avenue
Toronto, Ontario
M5G 2E9

Contents

Introduction

This anthology is the fourth in a series that includes *Poets of the Confederation*, *Poets Between the Wars*, and *Poetry of Mid-Century*. It follows its predecessors in its principle of selection, limiting itself to the representation of a few poets in depth, and since it does not intend to go over the ground covered by earlier volumes, particularly by *Poetry of Mid-Century*, its selection is confined primarily to poets whose work first appeared during the decade 1960-1970.

It should be clear at once that the boundaries of this volume have been drawn strictly and somewhat arbitrarily and that only in a very special sense can it claim to be representative of contemporary Canadian poetry. Poets, after all, do not produce poetry for the convenience of editors of anthologies. So long as they continue to write, they defy our critical wisdom, confound our attempts at precise description, and redefine not only the past of our literature but their own past as well. No one who read the earliest of Al Purdy's books could have foreseen his development as a poet, but any alert reader ought at least to have suspected that Purdy would not only metaphorically but literally revise the past. Only when the writer ceases to write does he offer something like a fixed point of reference, but even that is frequently a distant, wavering star, mysterious as a quasar, baffling our desire for certainty.

One difficulty, then, created by the arbitrary boundaries of this and earlier volumes in the series, is that by imposing forms and categories (even a category so ill-defined as "contemporary") on poetry, we distort a living form and do violence to the fertility and energy of our best writers. For the editor of *Poetry of Mid-Century*, the questions posed in making a selection were not only where to begin but where to stop. Now, some seven years later, the same puzzles remain to perplex the present editor. If my concern, for example, were, without qualification, to represent the best contemporary poetry published in Canada, I might want to revise and bring up to date the Milton Wilson selection. It would make as much sense, surely, to represent contemporary Canadian writing with new work by Irving Layton, Earle Birney, Raymond Souster, and Alden Nowlan (all of whom were included in *Poetry of Mid-Century*) as to choose, on principle, poets whose work has not previously appeared in this series. In fact, there is a compelling reason for believing that a writer such as Nowlan should be included in the present volume: much of his best work had not appeared at the time of Wilson's publication. Equally, given the new perspectives of the present, there might be an argument for including in a contemporary anthology the work of poets whose main publication thus far has been in the 1950's, but who seem now, for a variety of reasons, more interesting than when they first appeared.

Perhaps all this is simply to say that modern poetry in Canada extends in something like an unbroken line from at least the mid-1940's (wherever we place its beginnings) to the present. And it is precisely that continuity in development which creates the difficulty in drawing boundaries. Because the year 1960 does not in any proper sense mark off a significant turning point or stage of development, I suppose, one instinctively wants now to revise earlier anthologies in the process of creating new ones. But if one difficulty is delimiting the past, another appears at the opposite extreme, when we try to draw a boundary at the present. Assuming the principle of selection is that the poetry represented in this volume will have been for the most part published in the 1960's and not previously included in this series, the problem still is to choose among not only those poets who have amply demonstrated their range and power but among those still younger writers whose initial publication offers clear signs of exceptional talent or significant new possibilities in contemporary writing. On the whole, it seemed to me better to think of this volume as one more concerned with achievement than with "new directions," and to that extent it is retrospective rather than, as several new anthologies introducing new writers strive to be, prophetic. Still, it remains a matter of regret that much of the accomplishment of an earlier period and the excitement of what begins to look like the future cannot be represented here.

I have made one exception to the rule concerning writers previously included in this series. It seems to me inescapable that in Leonard Cohen's work the sensibility of the sixties finds not only its most elegant but its most representative voice: its self-deprecating irony, its sado-masochism, its lyricism, its theatricality, the odd mixing of triviality and nobility, shoddiness and niceties, its nostalgia, its visionary gleams. Cohen's enormous popularity, too, particularly among young readers, tells us something of a major culture and in the process its very character has changed. In no other poet of this time is that change so clearly revealed as in Cohen. From his first book in 1956 to his songs and recordings, his career reads so very much like a cultural history, it is virtually impossible to conceive of an anthology of this period that would omit his poems.

But reasoning about choices is ultimately a self-defeating process. Once I had been given an area in which to work, certain names came to me with a peculiar insistence for which there is no rational explanation that I can fasten upon. The poets I include here did not appear out of a box of index cards shuffled according to esoteric set of rules, as in a child's game. They were the first ones *present* to me, perhaps as those whose accomplishment, proficiency, and assurance, whose excellence, had made them as familiar to me as any other writer publishing now. It would be nice to believe standards were so unequivocal, but I think not. The fact is there are voices that insist on being heard and to whom with gathering excitement we listen.

Paradoxically, we do not choose the present; we are chosen by it, as we are chosen, say, by Milton Acorn whose presence in this decade could only be ignored by the most determined of committees, but not by any living poet or reader for whom passionate language and dedication to craft are matters of great import. Choice, for me at least, finally comes down to knowing that Al Purdy's off-handed manner has forever altered my own sense of the possibilities of rhetoric, and that after reading him I could not again ignore the ghosts of history, place, or family; it comes down to being haunted by the dark figures Gwen MacEwen evokes, shadow-maker and magician, or by the jagged edges of Margaret Atwood's imagery, the terrifying coolness of her language; it has to do with the entirely new-old sense of place, even of Calgary, that Bowering's tentative lines move one into, and with the uncanny feeling that in Newlove's stanzas, poetry *is* place. It is always to be aware of difference, strangeness, possibility in the work of Joe Rosenblatt, Michael Ondaatje, and bill bisset, each an individual seeking to become, in the words of one writer's description of bissett, "a full-time visionary."

This is not to see the poets as a group. Differences between them may well be more striking than any similarities. What they share in common, I suppose, is largely their emergence as poets during the 1960's and their continued presence in new publication. Yet I think it is worth noticing curious, if superficial, links between them: Atwood publishes an article on MacEwen's poetry; she reviews Purdy; Purdy reviews Atwood; Bowering's *Gangs of Kosmos* alludes cryptically to the "three people on the cover" and offers "special thanks . . . to Margaret Atwood for her helpful suggestions"; Purdy edits and introduces Acorn's selected poems; bissett's Blew Ointment Press includes the work of Atwood and Ondaatje, and John Newlove pops up as curt advisor to Purdy in Purdy's introduction to an anthology of young Canadian poets. Ondaatje writes a critical study of Cohen; Bowering, a study of Purdy. No need to introduce a conspiracy theory of poetic development. I take it these connections are neither stronger nor more mysterious than equally evident connections between these and other Canadian writers, and probably less significant than the links within, say, the *Preview* group or the *Contact* writers. Still, it might be worth thinking about what is common to their work, if not central to it, if for no other reason than the possibility that we might discover there some clues to that always unsolved mystery in Canada, the nature of our cultural history or at least its present form.

Those literary connections, superficial as they are, should remind us of the closeness of the literary scene in this country, the elaborate web of communication between poets in their magazines, presses, jobs, and books, the fact the bissett's Vancouver is not so very remote from Rosenblatt's Toronto, and that, like many other Canadian poets, Newlove, Atwood, Bowering have journeyed from west to east to link Calgary, Edmonton, Regina, Kamsack, Vancouver, Toronto, and Montreal. Journeys, in fact, are one of their main motifs, even esoteric ones like those in MacEwen's Egyptian poems or the island-hopping of Cohen and Purdy. Yet, mobile, technologically sophisticated, contemporary writers surprise us with a determined regionalism, another version of traditional Canadian concerns with the land, wilderness, the pervasive notion that an ill-defined terror of space defines the authentic Canadian sense of things. This interplay of cultivated literary awareness and an almost primitive feeling for place seems to me both characteristic and revealing of contemporary writers. On the one hand, these writers move with exceptional confidence into new areas with new approaches to place, space, time, and personality; on the other hand, in their concern with land and history they look back to the traditional preoccupations of Canadian poetry.

At its best, as in the radical humanism of Milton Acorn, contemporary poetry transcends regionalism and the myth of the land. Acorn's prophetic utterances, asserting a genuine self in love and anger, have far more to do with social justice than with the metaphysics of a northern vision. Yet as a carpenter and an Islander, Acorn is not one to relinquish his hold on particularities, even for the sake of a perfect political theory. Purdy remarks that certain of Acorn's poems "give the impression of infinite time" because of his delicately lingering attention to detail. If we are reminded of Archibald Lampman (improbable as that may sound), not the land but the self is mythic then. The opposite version of this appears to be the one we find in the poetry of Gwen MacEwen who, rather like Joe Rosenblatt, transforms myth into personality: for her, magicians with the powers of pharaohs and ancient gods inhabit the soul, while for Rosenblatt a modern bestiary and comic-book characters speak awful and wonderful truths about man's psyche. Both MacEwen's and Rosenblatt's models are obviously less immediately Canadian than gothic and romantic, products of esoteric learning. In both poets, explicit Jungian interests apparently account for a tendency to psychologize myth, but whether, as with Acorn, passion transforms and reveals within personality a metaphoric structure, or whether psychological symbols are sought as keys to the doors of perception, all three writers – Acorn, Rosenblatt and MacEwen – are rather historians of the soul than of a land.

A somewhat different use of gothic and romantic elements appears in Margaret Atwood's poems. Not only time but space takes on mythic form in her work, the contemporary world as well as the historical one becomes psychological symbol, and the war of the divided self provides an ultimate political metaphor. A museum is not only a human brain but the recapitulation of the self as evolutionary history and geologic time; a Canadian pioneer evokes the terrors of contemporary alienation; and the most prosaic object, as in a Bergman film, threatens the poet with horrid potentialities.

In the poetry of Purdy, Bowering, and Newlove, we find further variations on this theme of myth as history, history as myth. The most capacious poet of all, Purdy, discovers the bones of a mythology in Indian, Eskimo, and Lake Roblin story and experience. His imagination moves uneasily admidst skeletons of learning, lore, and memory, seeking always the eloquence of loss, ruin, and transience, the language of disappearing forms. For Bowering, as for Newlove, the bright land is the measure of speech and breath. Bowering's *Rocky Mountain Foot*, essentially a collection of lyrics, seeks to organize itself into documentary-myth or mythic-documentary, or at least the sort of mixed form that will so energize the poet's language that fact and legend will become numinously fused within the poem. And, in an extraordinary poem, "The Pride," John Newlove puts together in endlessly evocative lines story, verse, the land, and its people:

> Those are all stories;
> the pride, the grand poem
> of our land, of the earth itself,
> will come, welcome, and
> sought for, and found
> in a line of running verse . . .
>
> the knowledge of
> our origins, and where
> we are in truth,
> whose land this is
> and is to be.

With Newlove's "The Pride," as with his "Samuel Hearne," and Atwood's *Susanna Moodie* we can discern the major tonalities and forms of the contemporary writer's encounter with the land, with space, with locality, with history. It is not difficult to see here, as in Bowering's and Purdy's themes, concerns defined in Canadian writing as early as E. J. Pratt's first poems and elaborated in the work of writers from Patrick Anderson to James Reaney and Jay Macpherson. It is equally easy to see, especially in diction and imagery, how the contemporary style connects with the sparse urgency of the poetry of W. W. E. Ross and Dorothy Livesay. As always the temptation is to invoke a geographical determinism and to account for such literary connections by speaking of new versions of the land, the prairies, the north shore of Lake Superior, the backwoods of Ontario, the Arctic. But even granted the possibility of accounting for language and imagery in geographical and regional terms, it seems hardly credible that the sense of self and personality at the centre of the new poetry could be the creation of ignorant chance, alone. At the very least, it is apparent that a different sort of person (indeed almost a non-person) speaks in contemporary poems: laconic, ironic, self-deprecating, tentative, it is, compared with the aggressive ego of Layton's verse, the dancing personality in Birney's poems, or the ornately rhetorical presence of Klein, an absurdly diminished being. To the extent that contemporary writers can be distinguished from others within the Canadian tradition, it is this sense of self that provides the distinguishing mark.

It is easy enough to seek an explanation for the diminished, ironic self of contemporary poetry in sociological and psychological patterns of the kind that form a popular mythology: the radical decentralization of the self in Norman O. Brown's psychomania, for example, or the politicization of ego in R. D. Laing's paradoxical inversions of sanity and insanity. But whether contemporary social psychologists, or poets like Pound, Olson, and Creeley, provide the appropriate explanation, what is clear is that the disappearing self of the poetry of the sixties is related in some way to the sense that myth and history, like political and psychological metaphors, are interchangeable in new and disturbing ways.

Two extremes of metaphoric language, at least in the sense in which Leslie Fiedler construes them, are nostalgia and hallucination. These could be translated, it seems to me, into dream and nightmare, idyllic memory of home and immediate perception of the demonic in land or city. A good deal of Canadian poetry is polarized in this way; sometimes the polarization appears as a small-town or rural contrast with the city; in its most contemporary version, as in some of bissett's land tantras, it becomes the proletarianism of the commune or *Whole-Earth Catalogue* opposed to the imperialism of multi-national corporations, technology, and America; sometimes, as in Cohen's *Flowers for Hitler* and his poetic novel, *Beautiful Losers*, its form is an inversion of the usual values attached to notions like sanity and insanity, civilization and barbarism.

With this last device, we encounter a pervasive form of the tentative or decentralized self of contemporary poetry: its most rational and coherent speech takes on ominous undertones of incoherence while its ecstatic chants, tantras, phonemic splutters are presented in the vestements of illumination and truth. In the coolness of Atwood's language one is meant to sense the presence of a manic persona, just as in the uncertain incoherencies of Al Purdy's characters one hears not only the mutter of inarticulate anger but the mumblings of a distracted poetic creation. Michael Ondaatje's anatomy of a killer, *The Collected Works of Billy the Kid*, achieves the cold precision of a surgeon's knife, "a sane assassin, a sane assassin, a sane assassin," its most volcanic passages those in which the utmost degree of restraint is exercised. And with other, lovely rhythms, bissett's poetry moves toward elemental moments of pure sound, the ecstatic discovery, within the syllable, of universal recurrence.

Perhaps the ultimate temptation of the contemporary imagination is primitivism. It is an imagination that seeks to express itself in the minimal, in speech, design, personality, a spare poetry as laconic as form itself. And yet, like primitive art, it is capable of moments of pure extravagance, chanting hymns and prayers, elaborating pictures for the sake of the pictorial, wandering inconsistently and incoherently amidst the fragments of personality and history, mixing space and time like the colours of an impossible colourist. Its emblem might very well be the look of paranoid schizophrenia attributed to Susanna Moodie (and Canada) by Atwood or the equally psychotic glare of Ondaatje's Billy the Kid.

Ondaatje's left-handed, sinister killer describes an allegory of the contemporary imagination in its lust for death and sex, for exploded heads and dementia of disease and drugs, a poetry of politics, or politics of poetry. No longer pure, his work mixes genres – movies and pulp-magazines stories, fiction and documentary, poems and prose, pictures and print. And as it breaks apart all the conventions we have learned so carefully as the lesson of our humanism and its forms, it breaks inside our heads, asking us to take as the measure of our humanity the fantasies of a little boy. The book begins with a blank page, a photograph of the whiteness of the killer. It ends with a picture of a child in a cowboy suit. In between, is the imagination of contemporary poetry and of our own time.

Eli Mandel,
York University, 1971.

Al Purdy

After The Rats

Little by little I am diminishing . . .
After uneasy sleep I find
the rats have taken
a toe or finger, gnawed
a hole in me until I can
button my overcoat in flesh.

Sometimes I wonder
about my parts, what rodents do
with them: construct
a man in burrows, fill in
uncertain areas with fur that is
indistinguishable from me?

These rats – my dreams reveal
them, brown streams running
back and forth to check
my measurements, or compare
the fragment of soul that's left
me with the one they have
which has my blood on it.

In all this reasoning I favour
myself – when I impute
rats, and cannot prove
at all they really did and do exist.
Except each morning I see
myself lessen, diminish . . .
Frantically I cling
to heart tissue, tightly hold
the intangibility located
in my head where thoughts rush
out and charge and change and die.
It's curious. One would not think
habit of belief, custom of thinking,
syllogism, paradigm of me could
disappear and some other me
replace me some other silly mannikin
enact again my whole personal painful
joyful unique personality:

but I expect soon
to be sitting in a tavern drinking
beer contemplatively, and one by one
thirstily the other beasts enter.

1958

Gilgamesh and Friend

Eabani, alias Enkidu, made by an itinerant goddess
from clay – hairy, reasonably human,
destined to have carbuncles, lung cancer, fear of death –

Became friend of certain beasts, and notable in that
he learned their language (played the flute?),
left animals for a whore – uh, courtesan

(How'd she do it?). Joined Gilgamesh to initiate heroism
(first known ism?) in the Sumerian microcosm.
Killed bulls, wizards, monsters like Shumbaba

(who had no genitals, thank goodness) in a cedar forest,
judiciously aided by Bel, Aruru, and Shamah.
Thru the adolescent world these Sumerian tourists

made the happy scene. But Eabani died.
Girl-crazy Gilgamesh, pot-smoker, fame-seeker,
wept (took LSD?), troubled gods with sharp cries.

Sought Utanapishtim, the old ark navigator
from flood days, senile but certified immortal,
with snappy snarl asked him his life-recipe.

Denied. Gilgamesh, the tired folk hero
died, first mentioning to late-comer Assur-
bani pal the need of a stone tablet to commemorate

his natural modesty: laid down among jewellery,
brazen spears, piled armor, heard desert jackals whine
(grinned?), nipping heels of tearful concubines;

felt numbness, emptying, first slow tremor
of translation to another scene, became a story,
and went stammering into the centuries . . .

1959

The Listeners

"I might have married her once but
   being an overnight guest of hers changed my mind –"
A big man who looked like a truck driver,
   getting sober as you can get on beer,
   and he suddenly burst out with that –
"What happened?" I said.
"Her old man was dying of something or
   other in a room downstairs without
   drugs and screamed most of the time –
   I could see the line of light under her door,
   and I kept wanting and then not wanting
   her between yells. I'd hear the wind blow,
   the woodwork creak, and listen some more and
   think of the girl – then he'd scream."
The waiter came by with beer.

                  "Here," I said,
and paid him and grinned in the familiar friendly
   roar of the jammed full tavern and talk boomed
   in my ears –

           "Go on," I said.
"After midnight, me lying and listening,
   hearing people asleep and some not asleep,
   the sounds an old house makes to itself
   for company, the nails and boards and bricks
   holding together such a long time and knowing
   so many things about people

                       then he'd scream and
I'd say to myself, 'Go on an die, go on an die –'
   They must've had the windows open wide,
   for the sound came in from outside too.
   I'd hear the crickets and then he'd scream!
   Finally I heard the girl scramble out of bed,
   she came rushing into my room in a nightgown
   and dragged me downstairs and outside,
   holding my hand so hard she cut thru calluses,
   holding my hand and running like hell
   into the fields

              into the fields . . .
Oh it was good, I thought, it was fine,
   the silence and she wanting me and I –
But I looked and it wasn't wanting in her eyes,
   not wanting at all in her gray eyes

                  but waiting . . .
Migawd, what was she waiting for in that wheat field?

What did she want to make me do or say or be
suddenly there in the moonlight?
Well (he said defiantly), I wouldn't."
Reassurance seemed in order when I
looked at the big sweating red face and said,
"Nothing happened: you didn't make love,
the old man didn't die, you went away unchanged –"
He looked at me and the room grew silent,
as if everyone had been listening to his story,
at closing time around the upside down tables,
everyone listened still

                              everyone listened –

1961

On the Decipherment of "Linear B"

(By Michael Ventris and associates)

Grammatic structure first, then phonetic values:
Ventris mailing progress reports to philologists
for comment (by air across the Atlantic):
the endgame – all the dusty Cretan sibilants
hissing delightedly back to life on scholar tongues,
whispering possible gossip to the co-translators
– that turned out to be inventories,
amphorae in warehouses, wine long vanished,
dried to red dust in the guts of Mycenaean warriors;
listings of clergy reserves, military property:
"Horse vehicle, painted red, supplied with reins";
words, preserved like nothing machines make,
perfect, unflawed, the same.

We see them (dramatic as hell), the code-breakers,
in shirt sleeves, drinking gallons of coffee:
gowned Oxford dons, real estate brokers,
American academics – a linguistic orgy,
broken by twitterings of girlish excitement,
punctuated with cries of discovery.

It turns out Minos was maybe an expatriate
Greek, who said to hell with hiero-
glyphic symbols: brought in the smith Daedalus
(a bad mistake re Pasiphae's morals)
to promote Greek investment, Linear B and stud poker –
Well, anyway Ventris figured it out,
and anyone can sit down after work reading
comic books or Agamemnon's diaries now.

But Knossos did burn, its flaming windows
signalled the stars 3,000 years ago:
when men died foetal, rolled into blackened balls,
and women, abandoned by children and lovers,
fled to the palace upper rooms with skirts on fire:
and over the island a south wind blowing –

1958

Necropsy of Love

If it came about you died
it might be said I loved you:
love is an absolute as death is,
and neither bears false witness to the other –
But you remain alive.

No, I do not love you
                    hate the word,
that private tyranny inside a public sound,
your freedom's yours and not my own:
but hold my separate madness like a sword,
and plunge it in your body all night long.

If death shall strip our bones of all but bones,
then here's the flesh and flesh that's drunken-sweet
as wine cups in deceptive lunar light:
reach up your hand and turn the moonlight off,
and maybe it was never there at all,
so never promise anything to me:
but reach across the darkness with your hand,
reach across the distance of tonight,
and touch the moving moment once again
                    before you fall asleep –

5   Al Purdy

Mountain Lions in Stanley Park

(Vancouver, B.C.)

Canadian as the Winnipeg Gold-Eye or
the Calgary Eye-Opener and
regional in this province as Strontium 90 and
international as a boundary they
lived here before night's fuses were blown –

Remember the child?
                 He thought darkness had a nucleus
                              something plotting
outside his range of vision something
              that moved and shambled
              laughed without logic
              and drooled –
It's rather a comfort now
to see the caged cougar's
fierce eyes focused
                 serious
                        (non-idiotic) and
to be involved in the cougar's simple problems
(the snap of a bone in the head exchanging
                        light for darkness)
and walking to the edge of this floodlit concrete
not stopping at all
on the edge of the great trees –
Sun-coloured cougar
                 you have forgotten the past
in this managed place where the sky
is snugged down with green tent pegs
and buildings litter the landscape
like rubble and a river of animals
hoarsely pouring down the morning
into foglit factories
                 Remember quickly
the nature of boundaries –
And child of darkness
              remember the future
those strange beasts under the horizon
will want to ask questions
concerning your birthplace
                 require of you
reasons for departure
deny you entry to the walking forest

Say to them
         the name is unpronounceable
         but there will be other beasts
         where I am going
We will meet there –

Mice in the House

One of them scampers down the curtain
and up to my motionless feet –
I have the feeling watching that
representatives of two powerful races
are meeting here calmly as equals –
But the mouse will not be damn fool enough
         to go away and write a poem –

Home-Made Beer

I was justly annoyed 10 years ago
in Vancouver: making beer in a crock
under the kitchen table when this
next door youngster playing with my own
kid managed to sit down in it and
emerged with one end malted –
With excessive moderation I yodelled
at him
      "Keep your ass out of my beer!"
       And the little monster fled –
Whereupon my wife appeared from the bathroom
where she had been brooding for days
over the injustice of being a woman and
attacked me with a broom –
With commendable savoir faire I broke
the broom across my knee (it hurt too) and
then she grabbed the breadknife and made
for me with fairly obvious intentions –
I tore open my shirt and told her calmly
with bared breast and a minimum of boredom
      "Go ahead! Strike! Go ahead!"
Icicles dropped from her fiery eyes as she
snarled
      "I wouldn't want to go to jail
      for killing a thing like you"
I could see at once she loved me

tho it was cleverly concealed –
For the next few weeks I had to distribute
the meals she prepared among neighbouring
dogs because of the rat poison and
addressed her as Missus Borgia –
That was a long time ago and while
at the time I deplored her lack of
self control I find myself sentimental about
it now for it can never happen again –

Sept. 22, 1964. P.S. I was wrong –

The Country North of Belleville

Bush land scrub land –
      Cashel Township and Wollaston
Elvezir McClure and Dungannon
green lands of Weslemkoon Lake
where a man might have some
        opinion of what beauty
is and none deny him
              for miles –

Yet this is the country of defeat
where Sisyphus rolls a big stone
year after year up the ancient hills
picnicking glaciers have left strewn
with centuries' rubble
            days in the sun
when realization seeps slow in the mind
without grandeur or self deception in
        noble struggle
of being a fool –
A country of quiescence and still distance
a lean land
      not fat
with inches of black soil on
        earth's round belly –
And where the farms are it's
      as if a man stuck
both thumbs in the stony earth and pulled

                    it apart to make room
enough between the trees
for a wife
                    and maybe some cows and
                    room for some
of the more easily kept illusions –
And where the farms have gone back
to forest
                    are only soft outlines and
                    shadowy differences –
Old fences drift vaguely among the trees
                    a pile of moss-covered stones
gathered for some ghost purpose
has lost meaning under the meaningless sky
                    – they are like cities under water and
the undulating green waves of time are
                    laid on them –

This is the country of our defeat and
                    yet
during the fall plowing a man
might stop and stand in a brown valley of the furrows
                    and shade his eyes to watch for the same
                    red patch mixed with gold
                    that appears on the same
                    spot in the hills
                    year after year
                    and grow old
plowing and plowing a ten acre field until
the convolutions run parallel with his own brain –

And this is a country where the young
                    leave quickly
unwilling to know what their fathers know
or think the words their mothers do not say –

9   Al Purdy

Herschel Monteagle and Faraday
lakeland rockland and hill country
a little adjacent to where the world is
a little north of where the cities are and
sometime
we may go back there
                        to the country of our defeat
Wollaston Elvezir Dungannon
and Weslemkoon lake land
where the high townships of Cashel
                        McClure and Marmora once were –
But it's been a long time since
and we must enquire the way
                        of strangers –

To An Attempted Suicide

(At Sunnybrook Hospital)

What can I do for you
            my friend?
Will you try again soon?
Is the goddam world that desolate?
            – thrown away cigarette butts
            picked up by bums and
            people's lives nobody
            picks up –

This robbery of all you thought valuable
            committed in private
            committed by a woman
– isn't it maybe possible that such a theft allows
            unnoticed things of no value and
            visible for the first time to
Gleam
      gold
            in a chill sun?

(This curious creature
behind bars at a military zoo
watched closely by attendants
as the pendulum swings back and
forth between here and death
euphoria and black depression
alternating bouts with Jacob's angel
and the eyes of visiting spectators

swivel left and right for tennis tho
who wins arouses much disinterest and
someone says hell I'm interested –
But you can't prove it
              can you mister?)

You self pitying slob you
stupid bastard I can talk rings around (and
leave uncircled the silence of things) who
thought he was so irresistible women melted
under his loins after the words' boom was
always previously and primarily still there oh yes
            you roaring at the bourgeois
            or just ranting-silly and
            so beautifully –
I can love a man with such a splendid weakness
            for a woman
            crying jag for the world's
            hurt people and
            if I talk too fast
            blinded by arrogance
angry at all unchangeable things that happen
myself grown tired
            of the long
            humiliation of living
            nevertheless
will you please continue to stand there for a while
            with that dumb look
            of the world's enduring losers those
continual spendthrifts of their mortal selves
– stand somewhere in imagination's distance
            from your foolish dreams and
               halfway back to here from there
                 sustain me with your presence
                   – my friend?

Trees at the Arctic Circle

(*Salix Cordifolia* – Ground Willow)

They are 18 inches long
or even less
crawling under rocks
grovelling among the lichens
bending and curling to escape
making themselves small
finding new ways to hide
Coward trees
I am angry to see them
like this
not proud of what they are
bowing to weather instead
careful of themselves
worried about the sky
afraid of exposing their limbs
like a Victorian married couple

I call to mind great Douglas firs
I see tall maples waving green
and oaks like gods in autumn gold
the whole horizon jungle dark
and I crouched under that continual night
But these
even the dwarf shrubs of Ontario
mock them
Coward trees

And yet – and yet –
their seed pods glow
like delicate grey earrings
their leaves are veined and intricate
like tiny parkas
They have about three months
to ensure the species does not die
and that's how they spend their time
unbothered by any human opinion
just digging in here and now
sending their roots down down down
And you know it occurs to me
                    about 2 feet under
those roots must touch permafrost
ice that remains ice forever
and they use it for their nourishment
use death to remain alive

I see that I've been carried away
in my scorn of the dwarf trees
most foolish in my judgements
To take away the dignity
            of any living thing
even tho it cannot understand
            the scornful words
is to make life itself trivial
and yourself the Pontifex Maximus
            of nullity
I have been stupid in a poem
I will not alter the poem
but let the stupidity remain permanent
as the trees are
in a poem
the dwarf trees of Baffin Island

Pangnirtung

Innuit

An old man carving soapstone
at the co-op in Frobisher Bay
and in his faded eyes
it is possible to see them
shadowy figures
past the Dorset and pre-Dorset Cultures
5,000 years ago
if you look closely
But the race-soul has drawn back
drawn back
from settlements and landing fields
from white men
into secret vaults
and catacombs of marrow
bone rooms
that reveal nothing
The Innuit which is to say
            THE PEOPLE
as the Greeks called all foreigners
            barbaroi
something other than themselves
            un-GREEK
so the Innuit
            The People

13   Al Purdy

these unknowable human beings
who have endured 5,000 years
on the edge of the world
a myth from long ago
that reaches into the past
but touches an old man still living
Looking into his eyes
it is possible to see the first hunters
(if you have your own vision)
after the last ice age
moving eastward from Siberia
without dogs or equipment
toward the new country
pausing on the sea-ice
for a moment of rest
then pushing on thru the white smother
– Flying generations
leap and converge on this face
an old man carving soapstone
with the race-soul of The People
THE PEOPLE
moving somewhere
behind his eyes

Pangnirtung

Elegy for A Grandfather

Well, he died I guess. They said he did.
His wide whalebone hips will make a prehistoric barrow
men of the future may find and perhaps may not:
where this man's relatives ducked their heads
in real and pretended sorrow
for the dearly beloved gone thank Christ to God,
after a bad century: a tough big-bellied Pharaoh,
with a deck of cards in his pocket and a Presbyterian grin –

Maybe he did die, but the boy didn't understand it,
the man knows now and the scandal never grows old
of a happy lumberjack who lived on rotten whiskey,
and died of sin and Quaker oats age 90 or so.
But all he was was too much for any man to be,
a life so full he couldn't include one more thing,
nor tell the same story twice if he'd wanted to,
and didn't and didn't –

Just the same he's dead. A sticky religious voice
folded his century sideways to get it out of sight,
and lowered him into the ground like someone still alive
who made other people uncomfortable:
barn raiser and backwoods farmer,
become an old man in a one-room apartment
over a drygoods store –
And earth takes him as it takes more beautiful things:
populations of whole countries,
museums and works of art,
and women with such a glow
it makes their background vanish
                    they vanish too,
and Lesbia's singer in her sunny islands
stopped when the sun went down –

No, my grandfather was decidedly unbeautiful,
250 pounds of scarred slag.
And I've somehow become his memory,
taking on flesh and blood again
the way he imagined me,
floating among the pictures in his mind
where his dead body is,
laid deep in the earth –
and such a relayed picture perhaps
outlives any work of art,
survives among its alternatives.

Detail

The ruined stone house
has an old apple tree
left there by the farmer
whatever else he took with him
It bears fruit every year
gone wild and wormy
with small bitter apples
nobody eats
even children know better
I passed that way on the road
to Trenton twice a month
all winter long
noticing how the apples clung
in spite of hurricane winds
sometimes with caps of snow

15   Al Purdy

little golden bells
And perhaps none of the other
travellers looked that way
but I make no parable of them
they were there and that's all
For some reason I must remember
and think of the leafless tree
and its fermented fruit
one week in late January
when wind blew down the sun
and earth shook like a cold room
no one could live in
with zero weather
soundless golden bells
alone in the storm

Interruption

When the new house was built
callers came:
black squirrels on the roof every morning
between sleep and wakefulness,
and a voice saying "Hello dead man."
A chipmunk looks in the window
and I look out,
the small face and the large one
waver together in glass,
but neither moves
for the instant of our lifetimes.
Orioles, robins and red-winged blackbirds
are crayons that colour the air;
something sad and old
cries down in the swamp.
Moonlight in the living room,
a row of mice single file
route marching across the empty lunar plain
until they touch one of my thoughts
and jump back frightened,
but I don't wake up.
Pike in the lake pass and re-pass the windows
with clouds in their mouth.
For 20 minutes every night
the sun slaps a red paint brush
over dinner dishes and leftovers,
but we keep washing it off.

Birds can't take a short cut home,
they have to fly around the new house;
and cedars grow pale green candles
to light their way thru the dark.
Already the house is old:
a drowned chipmunk (the same one?)
in the rain barrel this morning
dead robins in the roof overhang,
and the mice are terrified –
We have set traps,
and must always remember
to avoid them ourselves.

Wilderness Gothic

Across Roblin Lake, two shores away,
they are sheathing the church spire
with new metal. Someone hangs in the sky
over there from a piece of rope,
hammering and fitting God's belly-scratcher,
working his way up along the spire
until there's nothing left to nail on –
Perhaps the workman's faith reaches beyond:
touches intangibles, wrestles with Jacob,
replacing rotten timber with pine thews,
pounds hard in the blue cave of the sky,
contends heroically with difficult problems
of gravity, sky navigation and mythopeia,
his volunteer time and labor donated to God,
minus sick benefits of course on a non-union job –

Fields around are yellowing into harvest,
nestling and fingerling are sky and water borne,
death is yodeling quiet in green woodlots,
and bodies of three young birds have disappeared
in the sub-surface of the new county highway –

That picture is incomplete, part left out
that might alter the whole Dürer landscape.
gothic ancestors peer from medieval sky,
dour faces trapped in photograph albums escaping
to clop down iron roads with matched greys:
work-sodden wives groping inside their flesh
for what keeps moving and changing and flashing
beyond and past the long frozen Victorian day.

A sign of fire and brimstone? A two-headed calf
born in the barn last night? A sharp female agony?
An age and a faith moving into transition,
the dinner cold and new-baked bread a failure,
deep woods shiver and water drops hang pendant,
double yolked eggs and the house creaks a little –
Something is about to happen. Leaves are still.
Two shores away, a man hammering in the sky.
Perhaps he will fall.

Lament for the Dorsets

(Eskimos extinct in the 14th century A.D.)

Animal bones and some mossy tent rings
scrapers and spearheads   carved ivory swans
all that remains of the Dorset giants
who drove the Vikings back to their long ships
talked to spirits of earth and water
– a picture of terrifying old men
so large they broke the backs of bears
so small they lurk behind bone rafters
in the brain of modern hunters
among good thoughts and warm things
and come out at night
to spit on the stars

The big men with clever fingers
who had no dogs and hauled their sleds
over the frozen northern oceans
awkward giants
                    killers of seal
they couldn't compete with little men
who came from the west with dogs
Or else in a warm climatic cycle
the seals went back to cold waters
and the puzzled Dorsets scratched their heads
with hairy thumbs around 1350 A.D.
– couldn't figure it out
went around saying to each other
plaintively
          "What's wrong? What happened?
            Where are the seals gone?"
And died

Twentieth century people
apartment dwellers
executives of neon death
warmakers with things that explode
– they have never imagined us in their future
how could we imagine them in the past
squatting among the moving glaciers
six hundred years ago
with glowing lamps?
As remote or nearly
as the trilobites and swamps
when coal became
or the last great reptile hissed
at a mammal the size of a mouse
that squeaked and fled

Did they ever realize at all
what was happening to them?
Some old hunter with one lame leg
a bear had chewed
sitting in a caribou skin tent
– the last Dorset?
Let's say his name was Kudluk
carving 2-inch ivory swans
for a dead grand-daughter
taking them out of his mind
he places in his mind
where pictures are
He selects a sharp stone tool
to gouge a parallel pattern of lines
on both sides of the swan
holding it with his left hand
bearing down and transmitting
his body's weight
from brain to arm and right hand
and one of his thoughts
turns to ivory
The carving is laid aside
in beginning darkness
at the end of hunger
after a while wind
blows down the tent and snow
begins to cover him
After 600 years
the ivory thought
is still warm

19   Al Purdy

Beothuck Indian Skeleton in Glass Case

(St. John's Museum, Nfld.)

Six feet three inches
a man of 40
and not made for crawling on
his belly surely
the sight of this walking sunset
must have amazed white pygmies
from fog-bound fishing villages
of Joe Batt's Arm and Famish Gut
before they tracked him down

He's the same height I am
which makes me speculate
he'd have the same bother
with low doorways and car seats
and keep bumping his head on things
never stand face to face with a girl
and have to lie down with her
to be properly friends
But that's as far as it goes
my death is some way off yet
and enemies blend with the landscape
I gawk at the gawking tourists
over this last symbol
of his extinct nation
consider the great auks and plants
of the remote carboniferous
and man-apes hitch-hiking towards a camera
I ought to feel sadness here
but can't
only a slight amazement
at the gawking tourists
that these specimens survived
and the man in the glass case didn't

Remains of An Indian Village

Underfoot rotten boards, forest rubble, bones . . .
Animals were here after the plague,
after smallpox to make another ending:
for the tutelary gods of decay
acknowledge aid from any quarter . . .

Here the charging cotyledons of spring
press green forefingers
on femurs, vertebrae, and delicate
belled skulls of children;
the moon's waylaid light does not shrink
from bone relics and other beauties of nature . . .

Death is certainly absent now,
at least in the overwhelming sense
that it once walked at night in the village
and howled thru the mouths of dogs –
But everything fades
and wavers into something else,
the seasonal cycle and the planet's rhythm
vary imperceptibly into the other;
spirits of the dead are vanished,
only great trees remain,
and the birth certificate of cedars
specifies no memory of a village . . .

(And I have seen myself fade
from a woman's eyes
while I was standing there,
and the earth was aware of
me no longer –)
But I come here as part of the process
in the pale morning light,
thinking what has been thought by no one
for years of their absence,
in some way continuing them –
And I observe the children's shadows
running in this green light from
                                    a distant star

into the near forest –
wood violets and trilliums of
a hundred years ago
blooming and vanishing –
the villages of the brown people
toppling and returning –
What moves and lives
        occupying the same space,
what touches what touched them
                                owes them . . .

21   Al Purdy

Standing knee-deep in the joined earth
of their weightless bones,
in the archaeological sunlight,
the trembling voltage of summer,
in the sunken reservoirs of rain,
standing waist-deep in the criss-cross
rivers of shadows,
in the village of nightfall,
the hunters silent and women
bending over dark fires,
I hear their broken consonants . . .

1961

Milton Acorn

I've Tasted My Blood

If this brain's over-tempered
consider that the fire was want
and the hammers were fists.
I've tasted my blood too much
to love what I was born to.

But my mother's look
was a field of brown oats, soft-bearded;
her voice rain and air rich with lilacs:
and I loved her too much to like
how she dragged her days like a sled over gravel.

Playmates? I remember where their skulls roll!
One died hungry, gnawing grey perch-planks;
one fell, and landed so hard he splashed;
and many and many
come up atom by atom
in the worm-casts of Europe.

My deep prayer a curse.
My deep prayer the promise that this won't be.
My deep prayer my cunning,
my love, my anger,
and often even my forgiveness
that this won't be and be.
I've tasted my blood too much
to abide what I was born to.

Non-Prayer

Dear old God, I'm not at odds with Thee;
I've got stronger friends
And more ferocious enemies –

If there's no God there's no atheist god either;
Nothing commands me to acts of villainy,
Nothing commands me to hate what doesn't exist . .
And is there a rule against loving It?

Poem for The Astronauts

As a wild duck painted sunrise colors
blurs his wings with speed
to a land known only to his heart's thrill
so man's truest home is the wind
created of his breath
and he breathes deepest in mystery.

New stars. Figures in the heavens.
Voices. How full
must be the vessel, the eye
that searches emptiness!

Canada is the scent of pines.
I left my land and returned
to know this and become Canadian.
To be an earthman I must leave Earth:
And what is Earth?
The whisper of grass?

Seeds turbulent
with fearful exultance
voyaging . . .

An Indian running the desert
kept a stone under his tongue
to drink the saliva, and
his skin remembered a thousand light touches
– fingers of his beloved.

Poem Poem

Yesterday a bust of breath
Poems broke from the white dam of my teeth.
I sang truth, the word I was;
And with each shout curling my tongue
Heart and fist thumped together.

But the poem I write today grins
While I chop it like a mean boy,
And whittles my spine.
Insinuating friend or stranger
It is truth, the word I am not.

The Plunge

Underneath muscles bloodrich and woven
my bones shake
to suddenly know myself beloved
by you, strong and all of a woman.

That word love only tickles
my lip between giggles
until you sing
my name calling me to stand tall
... and that's a swaying thing.

I feel a jolly decorated male bee
about to explode in love's shudder,
like going up in a highspeed elevator
with no floor – only handholds.

But let down your hair, love; let it down
so it hangs low as my navel;
and I'll hold on love, hold on
till we hop all tangled in joy
the whole length of Hell.

In Memory of Tommy, An Orphan, Who Was Kidnapped from His Loving Foster-Mother, Katherine, in Fulfillment of A Bargain Between Churches

No wonder the boy dreamt of monsters
terrible in horns, mooing his name,
chasing to tickle and eat him; no wonder
these drownpools of eyes looked in
the second storey window, their bland face
brooding cruel grown-up abstractions;
no wonder that dinosaur with the cooing
dove voice, too big to hide in a barn:
no wonder he woke with terror caught
like a fishbone in his throat, to huddle
amidst a dark full of faces.

I don't know if hate's the armer of love;
what side he joined, or if he joined: but
when he learned to hate those dreams ended.

In Addition

In addition to the fact I lost my job for a nosebleed

In addition to the fact my unemployment insurance stamps were just
    one week short

In addition to the fact I'm standing in line at the Sally Ann for a
    breakfast of one thin baloney sandwich and coffee

In addition to all that it's lousy coffee.

Belle

Younger, Belle was lonely, but now
the men brandish forearms in her kitchen,
shake themselves out with laughter.
The wives, glad they're not at mischief,
respect her jet black mane from a distance.

Edwin with his glasses, his pipe,
and freckled, spare-tipped fingers,
she married at twenty-nine, had to
(everyone had to, but she
claims that weakness like a certificate),
hums to himself, makes
the best cider in the settlement, hangs
doors that open to one hooked finger,
says four words in a day
and two of them are "No Ma'am!"

There's a contest of daughters
and one son,
born beside a mare munching clover.
She bore it alone,
herself whacked it into life.

Islanders

Would you guess from their broad greeting,
witty tuck of eyelids,
how they putt-putt out with lunch-cans
on sea liable to tangle
and dim out the land between two glances?

Tho their dads toed the decks of schooners,
dodging the blustery rush of capes,
and rum-runner uncles used wit-grease
against the shoot-first Yankee cutters,
they wouldn't be the kind to sail their
        lobster-boats around the world
for anything less than a dollar-ninety an hour.

1956

July Creatures

After the dim blue rain
swarms of innocent flying things
(green things, curly-bodied things,
things shaped like an arrowhead)
tiny with outsize wings

go wherever the wind wobbles
among pinwheeling swallows
and meet uncomprehended harm
in blond thickets on my forearm.

In The Thief's Mindseye

In the thief's mindseye our bright places
are photograph grey, and our darknesses
ways lit by his narrow intense want.

The conjurer too knows fissures in our vision
and there slips his deuces, discovers rabbits:
for it's by our needs we explore
and only become aware of shadows
when there's already a little light.

Scientists have been hoodwinked
by an old black-shawled woman, despising her
and unable to guess or believe
that a room has extra corners
a peasant can brood about and find before they.

27   Milton Acorn

The Idea

It's events itch the idea
into existence. The clawing
pixilating world lofts
the mind and its wrangling images
as contrary, gusty, circling
winds toss, flaunt the flags
(splendrous as if living) of
old duchies, unforgotten empires.

Then something palpable as voltage,
maybe a grim preacher, maybe
a wild thin man on a soapbox,
or even a character lugging
a pail and whitewash brush
(whitewash or smear it's all
a point of view) takes charge:
something you want in a way
savage or happy, takes charge;
the idea grows flesh, with nerves
to feel the pain of dismemberment.

But its life is death, and life's
going back to the chewing
creation obeying just itself;
so the herded clouds, dream-beasts
in the eyes' pasture, are torn
to fall like tears, like blood.
Then the idea's more like blood,
something in time with running feet,
with typewriter, with heartbeat.

Knowing I Live in A Dark Age

Knowing I live in a dark age before history,
I watch my wallet and
am less struck by gunfights in the avenues
than by the newsie with his dirty pink chapped face
calling a shabby poet back for his change.

The crows mobbing the blinking, sun-stupid owl;
wolves eating a hamstrung calf hindend first,
keeping their meat alive and fresh . . . these
are marks of foresight, beginnings of wit:

but Jesus wearing thorns and sunstroke
beating his life and death into words
to break the rods and blunt the axes of Rome:
this and like things followed.

Knowing that in this advertising rainbow
I live like a trapeze artist with a headache,
my poems are no aspirins . . . they show
pale bayonets of grass waving thin on dunes;
the paralytic and his lyric secrets;
my friend Al, union builder and cynic,
hesitating to believe his own delicate poems
lest he believe in something better than himself:
and history, which is yet to begin,
will exceed this, exalt this
as a poem erases and rewrites its poet.

To a Cockroach

Itsel ting, thee gives me a big wish
for words in some wee chir-
ped language

Since in the shaaaaaaa-
dow of Earnie's foot, thee stopped
and thy feelers all flit-flutter
went swiftly

not as if thee heared the high distractions
we bowled back and between us;
no – test-tastily thee
widdled the air, an so so so so

sharp thy wittle concern-things
touch-trembled thee . . . I see
how thee's got Earnie (old
bullet-in-the-brain-him Earnie) who

thee so pestify
all so absurdily tilted with love.

Tears the Dew of Beauty's Mourning

Thinking of a dove I have never seen
– tobacco leaf feathers, incense smoke and cream,
Eyes that bob black walking, in startled take-off;
Circles those eyes describe in the flutter roar, whisper and whistle
Of wings – shadows and shadow colors of thought and the world:

That there is no mourning in the dove, not in its cry
Except in the thought of it there's the thought of tears
Tiny and plump, as things living, running down shadowed face flesh;
And in tears, especially quiet ones, all things take beauty's texture . . .

I've cursed death as the realest face of God
– black finger swallowing the buttercup, shadow deeper
Than all the underness of waves; in the tap of that finger
     . . . vanishment.
The priest in black and gold of all his robed belly
Threatened death as all the pain-grey flashes
Of the worst of life, as life continuous –
A scream in which the throat's continually torn, fragmented
     and reborn –

But when I was thirteen Confucius appeared in a quotation
And dream as two merry eyes over a beard like sun and moon
     over the woodsey world;
Saying: – "Not know life . . . How know death?" And silent
As a foetal smile his laugh has grown in what you might call my soul.

I've thought of death as an ambiguous flavor, the swiftest taste
Which dissolves as you wonder what it's like –
As light fleeing from the last star on the edge of the universe
Its curving wave-front as wings, no eyes behind,
No brother-light or thought of light in front, no thought;
As the tongue-lick of a purring lioness . . .

And conversely I've denied with less fear than I've denied
My oh-so-bragging, oh-so-punishing Lord, that death's ever more real
Than now when my atoms are showering about me
     popping like raindrops
– that my headstone exists, that any particular moment exists
Sitting like that stone atop my twin gems, serpent eyes
On the head of my patterned trail through time; that anything
     true now
Will still be true on any day in which I will not die.

And yet again I've thought, "I will die . . ."
No fear . . . The priest's threat was life, not death;
Survival of only part of me, my pain, survival of myself as pain
Only, and every part of me become pain, life
Screaming my wounded name forever and ever
As he had already made me scream it:
This is what I feared, and it's gone
Except in my negating laugh, a little gold flower
Plucked and falling over and over in light wind ripples . . .

In these days before any of Time's old unthought evils
Dies, it incarnates itself
In a human body, in a brain and spit-slurring tongue
To scheme and argue its eternity:
That there are evil men; that they are evil
May hurt the mind with its truth, but
I predict their deaths, not mine:
And this thought is my comfort –

No fear . . . But like a little patch of violet
On a calling dove's throat (some imaginary species)
Mourning . . . I've wept for myself
As a laughing child, like the son I've lost, all the lost children –
Pronouncing their names as they're pronounced on my home island:
Out of the mouth as out of a bell;
And the waves of a south blue sea have lapped the roots of my lashes
As if they were forested shores

Tonguecut Prints of a Child Mouth as Birds

(To be read with windfire eyes)

The child singer in a cloud on the mountain
Troubles my thoughts of living things – their hearts, and roses
                                                    pale-blue:
His smile's mouth with wings beating stanzas like birds in flight –
Darkens and lightens with flying-out music . . .

Now his lips shape a gull wheeling across trapezoidal beams – the
                                              sun drawing water
As fishermen say . . . drinking of its pool of tears
To cry again, with joy at its daily happenstance, blessing land
With its tears, the creatures of its vision . . .
Gull turning with a terribly egocentric cry,
Plumage a vicious white turning black in the etched distance;
Spore of the sun as the child is . . .

31   Milton Acorn

Another verse and the child mouth curves again
Into a shape swift as a dove, blue in the chilling mist;
But his heart quick as a dove's heart knows little of the cold
And has no thoughts except of love
For the dove's the latest offspring of Creation
– later than men, almost brainless,
Flies well and knows its home, is first and last the worker
Of patterns in love, the dances of love, linked beaks and sounds of
                    love sewn into fabric of Time and the Earth . . .

And will he be the survivor? animicule with no anguish
Who'll watch the sun swell monstrously? unknowing
What suns are? why light becomes red?
Whose eyeballs'll become twin pygmy roses as the light becomes red?
Feathers the faint pink which'll be the white of those days?
And die in pairs singing of love
Til ice catches fragile throats?

But the child sees that terror – wings of his lips flap like
                    crows
And his voice becomes a "KAW" . . . a want, a will
To live! His song wills it harder and his lips become a raven
Devouring intense fragments of living matter in the deadly North;
Scheming how to live becomes wiser;
Seeds the egg with wisdom, becomes wiser,
Birth by rebirth becomes wiser –
Til his firey mirthful eye sets on the sun
Takes as into a beak its red pepper ball and his voice grown
                    terribly wise and fiercely sweet in the long ages
Calls the sun's new name and lights it again . . . !

The child sways like sapient wood in the mind – his mouth gets
                    round as an O
In mist curling away like the beard of a dying God . . . His
                    mouth's like a hollow
Nest in a swinging tree : tongue darts out
And in, out again like the red head of a nestling both fearful
                    and curious . . .
One last long note rises to High C – the cloud parts, *the
                    sky's dizzy with swallows* . . .
Til suddenly his voice breaks, sputters like an old volcano
. . . and the birds are frightened.

The Assassination of Kennedy

Truthful men lack that permanent pose
, feet rooted, cocks and guns
ready to shoot right and left
as chance calls it. Liars
stand like that
but the winds we soar in
eventually rip out their roots.

I swear I feel something
of the poet's exultation,
tho lately I've been sticking my head
out a door or window
to cry

not for him or his accused killer
. . . impossible to tell exactly who for
there are so many ones . . .
tho in talking about them
I'm cold and clever.

Each morning I shave myself
with the razor of my calculations
– nicked or not, hoping
the new face in the mirror
will be innocent;

so by minute and by year
I've gained an incredible assurance
. . . maybe fating me one day to be led out
, an "*arrogant red*," smiling
in the teeth of their final lie
Death . . .

The slamming shout of a bullet
smashes sift matter, sudden
night crashes in on a brain.

Poem

You'll climb or fall from this moment
, from this ledge you're on, naked
between the clouds, with the peak
invisible, and the valley you came from.

But should the eagle come now, wild
to rip the muscles around your heart,
here you must defend, even find some
of the things you want to realize.

You are, and you've got to prove it . . . you are
and it's a collective of proofs, like rocks
to build a cairn with; and what if you are
in the end, not yourself, but the proofs?

Pastoral

That sudden time I heard
the pulse of song in a thrush throat
my windy visions fluttered
like snow-clouds buffeting the moon.

I was born into an ambush
of preachers, propagandists, grafters,
("Fear life and death!" "Hate and pay me!")
and tho I learned to despise them all
my dreams were of rubbish and destruction.

But that song, and the drop-notes
of a brook truckling thru log-breaks and cedars,
I came to on numb clumsy limbs,
to find outside the beauty inside me.

Joe Rosenblatt

Breakfast I

Two hours ago I had devoured
scrambled eggs and bacon
but not with half the rapacity
of this spider-epicurean
I see eating a fly
on a thready napkin
to a point beyond
               psychotherapy.

Breakfast II

Nijinsky's spirit dances over
on eight spritely legs
towards the cosmonaut
glued on a parachute
and I become
a breakfast
for a dancer.

The Easter Egg I Got For Passover

*The body of Christ did not go to heaven, the moderator of the
United Church of Canada said yesterday. Right Rev. Ernest
Marshall Howse told a press conference that he does not believe in
the physical resurrection of Jesus, but does believe in a spiritual
resurrection. . . .*   —Toronto Globe & Mail. *April 23, 1965*

. . . . so much pain around the Easter egg, the Easter egg! the Easter egg! with
paschal scenes around the Easter egg; spikes, lilies & fallen angels inscribed,
in Persian space around the Easter egg; and the ladder, the safety ladder,
miraculously, held up by air (painted blue). And now this figure dressed in a
cloud suit climbs out of the ground looking as though he'd slept there for
several days on a uranium mattress, because he's all radiant, even his gown,
which is spotless. He climbs the safety ladder, the ladder that keeps leaning
against the sky. He climbs the ladder, sleepy, tired, maybe he's been on dex-
idrine, because he's haggard, bent over, like some of those characters I've
seen around the Village, walking the espresso mile. The bearded man keeps
scaling the ladder with a most violent headache; burning disc orbiting like
a hummingbird around his skull. Still haggard and bent, he progresses up the
ladder, now and then assisted by two sexless angels who act as his bufferin.

He stumbles up the ladder, the clouds are directly ahead (painted white); below, at the base of the ladder, a pastoral mob, shepherds & lambs & albino doves are sprinkled in the area. Now the audience is awed, stoned by this whole business. Imagine! a man climbing to heaven, without even a para-chute! Au revoir! We'll miss you on earth. Yes, send us a thunderbolt when you've made it. And the air keeps holding up the ladder. There's something wrong with this egg I got for Passover. I'm going to send it back, but there's no return address on the egg, the egg I got for Passover, the egg with so much pain painted around its belly. I'm going to knock on the egg. I'm going to find who has sent me this egg . . . Knock! . . Knock! . . No answer . . Knock! Knock! No answer? Knock! Knock! Knock! . . No answer, but a hand reaches through a crevice, and the hand drags the ladder through the crevice.

The Mole

The pink snouted mole,
inches of sleek fur night,
returned to the jaws –
a repeated trophy
for the Siamese cat.
Teeth clenched
the mole's smooth neck
and I who absorbed the drama,
knew the meaning of hell.
The blind squealing thing fled
beneath the cottage steps
as for the huntress –
she was bored, and
attacked the flies.

Jealousy

There is an orang-utan inside of me
and he jumps excitedly
when you throw your piranha eye
at me with scorpion's affection.
Take me apart,
one onion skin at a time,
only please don't
whittle me away with your eye
as you would
a hunk of wood.

Heliotrope

Heliotropism: The tendency of certain plants or other organisms
to turn or bend under the influence of sunlight.)

In the hospital ward
you react to sunlight
lifting your fingers every hour
to trap the helio flies –
as they hover above
the burning oranges on the table.
And now, with each hour moving
like a slow camel
in the dryness of your bones,
you observe
how every object in the room
is still like clay –
only you turning
as a heliotrope
in a flower pot

Metamorpho I

                        Lately I've become religious about atoms
and this is how I've come to dig the element man,
Metamorpho, freak with a 103 personalities
                        -the do-it-yourself chemistry set –
like
        . . . "don't get tough with me baby . . or I'll explode!"
grrrrr . . . I'm hydrogen
                I'm hydrofluoric acid . . . hssssss . .

I make pretty bubbles . . . I react with zinc

                          I'm a real base character

but Christ, NO! I am not Prince Metamorpho, nor was meant to be,
ugly and priceless, working myself into an atomic warhead,
a gold brick, a platinum egg . . . priceless . . .
poets give off so much laughing gas, but not Metamorpho
who comes on in metal metaphors: aluminum, copper and cobalt;
chases his tail with a tungsten tool, losing atomic weight
and burning up like phosphorus

                      before he flips his molecules
                      into an osmium

                                omelette

Uncle Nathan, Blessed Be His Memory, Speaketh From Landlocked Green

Wide, wide are the margins of sleep
deep, deep, deep in the flowerbox earth
I sleep . . . sleep . . . sleep . . .
In Carp's ethereal tabernacle
micron lips crackle
spirit embryos gestate
grow jinx wings, umbilical fins, slit gills
cold heart, lung, and lizard's spine
as from a cyanide backbone
flux of shadows strum . . . spiritons
from Death's encrusted harp piano.
Nephew, in this vibraic world
no dust remains, no nickle photos of our bones.
We are beyond dust
where spiritons and atoms hum
eloping with a perfect planetary sun
– such is spectral sex in the epicycle;
what red astronaut can match our mileage
revolve with us around the astral nucleus?
From worm to fluorescent penetrant
in the grave we all swing polar umbra.
Oye, so vengeful is Death's metamorphosis
that I go reincarnated in a minnow's whisper
who once dwelt orbicular in barbaric fishmonger;
and now who can measure my sad physique

                      . . . Givalt! . . . in a spectrogram?

or catch my printed whisper in a spectrograph?
Yet, more soul pinching than worm's acetylene,
no commerce is there in the Netherworld.

Earth Momma, forgive me for malicious filicide
for every fish I disembowelled was a child;
there is no Kaddish for aborted caviar.
Earth! Earth! is the bitch still green
liced with people and Aardvark powers?
And my shop on Baldwin Street
does she stand? . . . damp and sacred as the Wailing Wall
under the caterpillar'd canopy of God;
or has my pterodactyl neighbour
mogulled up my carp shrined Enterprise
wherein I cradled images from Lake Genneserat
to fish fertiled ladies with halvah tongues
who shred my serpents into shrimp bread,
for fish food oscillates an old maid's chromosomes!
Carp, pickerel, transmogrified,
such is the incantation of Gefilte Fish,
where swimmers have been tranquillized
stomach's the body's palpitating madrigal.
God, bless the primate's primeval stretch
but O to touch . . . touch . . .
a moon's vibration of a silver dollar
to see the fish scales rise and fall
before Lent's locust of Friday's carnivores.
Nephew, heaven is on earth; above me
the sky is smiling like a White Fish.
Its eyes are the moon and the sun.

And God said, "Let the waters bring forth swarms of living creatures,
and let birds fly above the earth across the firmament of the heavens."
Genesis

A Salmon Dying

This silver pickled salmon with rind smile gills lipping oxygen
he, Tarzan, pre-man is caught in wash web.

> Cells break down
> sleep is a sun
> we orbit then.

"Only a salmon dying," Larry had said,
eyes gunning telegraph line.
Fish were biting . . . concentrate . . . concentrate . . .
Then, flapping my arms, I, Anubis, ran along the sand bar jackalling.

39   Joe Rosenblatt

In the Fraser slapping, Cohoe Noah was dying (a cheek under
twenty pounds)
MASSIVE, even in death; domino black radar eyes zeroing zeroing.
Death was approaching. Approaching. I reached out. He was fog, and

Across the river
                    tufted in parsley of lime green forest
                    the pulp mill closed its sexual energy.

Dinner time: I waited for the fish to die, and the tide like a cat's lyric
                    tongue lapped liquid to sand playing bird with milk spittle
                    Fish vowel mouth ballooned. I paused.
                    There was some resemblance . . . Uncle Nathan?
                    Spirit, you ovulate more symbols than the Virgin Mary.

Water was cold. brrrrrrrr . . . Christ was really a fish.
I imagined dying in a cocktail.
There are the finest Swiss nerves in an olive.
And the eye
            being an eye
            can not see
                        computers.
In an olive
God's green voice is microscopic
as green is song
of growth in vertical

                    Cells break down
                    we orbit then.
I saw the shrew Apache of death
enter the pink poem mouth
of the salmon tumbling tumbling

                        salt drunk with D.T. pectoral fingers
                                                    convulsing.

Concentrate . . . concentrate . . . close your eyes, sorry you're dying.
How many sardines do you archetype . . . three?
Do you see twelve salmon eggs on twelve supper plates?
In relationship to the sum of all conscious being
                                    who. are. you.

                    you are an old man in a dry month.

            gulls . . . gulls . . . no, I won't let them

            even a fish deserves a Jewish burial.

The Painted Bird

Proboscis probing

                    "the painted bird," the oriental bat

is high on perfume.

                    Radar ears bend

gnomes are near with Cyprus nets.

                They pass by a sleeping apricot.

The Butterfly Bat

(for Selma Brody)

Bat Christ un-diurnal

                    cruci fix iated

                        in

                          honeycombed lettucy leafing wings.

tit bit optic ears twich twich twich.

You are a folding bat flower bearing a central mouse pod blot blind
under bloooom spunnnngery curtains veining rivulets of artery and
bloodvesseled monk transparent cells.
BUTTER butter BUTT but er FLY
BUTTERLY Butter fluttering fluttering flittering flitter··
flit flit flit flit flit flit flit flit flit flit flit flit FLIT

```
              w
   w          O              w
      w      wmw        w
       w   w          w   w
          w          w
```

Cerebellumbed & claw pawed in camouflage

a dark latexy tulip is daysleep

                 is Icarusy mouse petalfolding.

Happiness is a BUTTERflyMOTH

                    with wiggily thinning tail in Spider
                    warm webbing leaf.

as "FUH" is happiness in Chinese

                  Selma, I give you this gift, this

                         unhappily

                         LOve Poem

The Electric Rose

It sat in a Chinese garden
drinking the daylight.
"Get out of the way," it whispered,
"you're stealing my sunshine . . . my photons . . ."
An optical illusion, I concluded
as the obscene lips of the rose
closed.

I watched the rose glow:
its body was a crucible of fire
and its stamens . . . electrodes!
The redolence of the bud
held me in a molten trance
till a rustle at my feet
drew my eyes over to some weeds
sneaking up like green landlords.
"Save me!" cried the rose,
"they've been after me for weeks."
"Okay BUDDY, what's your name?"
"PHOTOSYNTHESIS," said the rose.
"Go on . . . you're putting me on," I replied.
"Hurry . . . PLEASE . . ." cried the rose,
"they're tickling my root hair!"
I reached for its throat.
"Get the roots . . . the roots . . . you silly rose beetle!"
Burrowing my fingers into the ground
I found the root
along with a broken finger nail.
"Easy . . . pull . . . gently," said the rose.
As I extracted the rose
from out of the ground
a mob gathered around my feet:
I was suddenly Daniel in the lions' den.
"Give us the rose," demanded the stranglers.
The verdant Mafia in their yellow sombreros
were crying for blood
but I would not appease the dandelions.
The rose collapsed in my hand
mob shocked and pale.
I carried it up to my room
where I mended the broken root
with iodine and band-aids.
In gratitude, the rose electric
beamed like a Bessemer converter
and recited a poem
from Li Po.

The Black Flower

It is a black flower
a flower without fragrance
detached like Death –
that small limbed girl
with silver hair
who in cosmetic consciousness resides –
narcist limboed in a glacial world.

I extend perception, perceive
aesthetic organism spinning
geodesic lines – filaments of love –
until, caught in a swoon of sensitive labour,
the spider lies exhausted on its back
and changes to that special flower
with eight tall stamen legs.

Marian

(who catch D frost)

Marian all mousetips & love lepsy
perspires peach perfumeries.
Silk spideries her filose thighs
eggcurvic her belly's mouse-in-milks –
invites snail's surf tung to tickle;
freckles are glad gland fish
in the penitentaries of her skin.

Sex lignites Christ lichen on her hands:
micefish, from O, so ocelots of loveheats
are seasons planted on calyculous cups.
O me'how you catch reindeerums.
Marian, delirim is not a sin
where inner obloong folding doors
are caterpillarcoated.

Cathedrals sob in Edelweiss
nectar's mistletoe exsbuds, exsploods
in vibrafooms of kinetic snow . . . .
D dying crouch on rocking thighs
& dew, Marian, are volooms
                              volooms of melting

Better She Dressed in a Black Garment . . .

A cold miserable nun's cell is her heart
and better she dressed in a black garment
for there's something beautiful in symmetry
of light and darkness, even though piety . . .
is the fang's invitation to a cobra.

Plagued by a prophecy before time's invention
when a protozoan held the first spring time
of Adam and Eve and parted the curse,
communion of flesh and blood found paradise
in its own image, but my hunger works it pain
like a white worm thru a red rose . . .
better she dressed in a black garment
concealing the flesh that is its own love.

Sun Poem

The sun
a peeping Tom
got his eyelids
thru the window
and brushed my desert brow.

I leaped
from the grave of a bed
and bolted the venetian blinds down
like guillotine.
Part of his eyelids fell on the floor.
I'll sweep them up soon.

45   Joe Rosenblatt

Leonard Cohen

Lovers

During the first pogrom they
Met behind the ruins of their homes –
Sweet merchants trading: her love
For a history-full of poems.

And at the hot ovens they
Cunningly managed a brief
Kiss before the soldier came
To knock out her golden teeth.

And in the furnace itself
As the flames flamed higher,
He tried to kiss her burning breasts
As she burned in the fire.

Later he often wondered:
Was their barter completed?
While men around him plundered
And knew he had been cheated.

Letter

How you murdered your family
means nothing to me
as your mouth moves across my body

And I know your dreams
of crumbling cities and galloping horses
of the sun coming too close
and the night never ending

but these mean nothing to me
beside your body

I know that outside a war is raging
that you issue orders
that babies are smothered and generals beheaded

but blood means nothing to me
it does not disturb your flesh

tasting blood on your tongue
does not shock me
as my arms grow into your hair

Do not think I do not understand
what happens
after the troops have been massacred
and the harlots put to the sword

And I write this only to rob you
that when one morning my head
hangs dripping with the other generals
from your house gate

that all this was anticipated
and so you will know that it meant nothing to me.

Go By Brooks

Go by brooks, love,
Where fish stare,
Go by brooks,
I will pass there.

Go by rivers,
Where eels throng,
Rivers, love,
I won't be long.

Go by oceans,
Where whales sail,
Oceans, love,
I will not fail.

I Have Not Lingered in European Monasteries

I have not lingered in European monasteries
and discovered among the tall grasses tombs of knights
who fell as beautifully as their ballads tell;
I have not parted the grasses
or purposefully left them thatched.

I have not released my mind to wander and wait
in those great distances
between the snowy mountains and the fishermen,
like a moon,
or a shell beneath the moving water.

I have not held my breath
so that I might hear the breathing of God,
or tamed my heartbeat with an exercise,
or starved for visions.
Although I have watched him often
I have not become the heron,
leaving my body on the shore,
and I have not become the luminous trout,
leaving my body in the air.

I have not worshipped wounds and relics,
or combs of iron,
or bodies wrapped and burnt in scrolls.

I have not been unhappy for ten thousand years.
During the day I laugh and during the night I sleep.
My favourite cooks prepare my meals,
my body cleans and repairs itself,
and all my work goes well.

As the Mist Leaves No Scar

As the mist leaves no scar
On the dark green hill,
So my body leaves no scar
On you, nor ever will.

When wind and hawk encounter,
What remains to keep?
So you and I encounter,
Then turn, then fall to sleep.

As many nights endure
Without a moon or star,
So will we endure
When one is gone and far.

For Anne

With Annie gone,
Whose eyes to compare
With the morning sun?

Not that I did compare,
But I do compare
Now that she's gone.

Out of the Land of Heaven

(for Marc Chagall)

Out of the land of heaven
Down comes the warm Sabbath sun
Into the spice-box of earth.
The Queen will make every Jew her lover.
        In a white silk coat
Our rabbi dances up the street,
Wearing our lawns like a green prayer-shawl,
Brandishing houses like silver flags.
        Behind him dance his pupils,
Dancing not so high
And chanting the rabbi's prayer,
But not so sweet.
        And who waits for him
On a throne at the end of the street
But the Sabbath Queen.
        Down go his hands
Into the spice-box of earth,
And there he finds the fragrant sun
For a wedding ring,
And draws her wedding finger through.
        Now back down the street they go,
Dancing higher than the silver flags.
His pupils somewhere have found wives too,
And all are chanting the rabbi's song
And leaping high in the perfumed air.
        Who calls him Rabbi?
Cart-horse and dogs call him Rabbi,
And he tells them:

The Queen makes every Jew her lover.
And gathering on their green lawns
The people call him Rabbi,
And fill their mouths with good bread
And his happy song.

The Genius

For you
I will be a ghetto jew
and dance
and put white stockings
on my twisted limbs
and poison wells
across the town

For you
I will be an apostate jew
and tell the Spanish priest
of the blood vow
in the Talmud
and where the bones
of the child are hid

For you
I will be a banker jew
and bring to ruin
a proud old hunting king
and end his line

For you
I will be a Broadway jew
and cry in theatres
for my mother
and sell bargain goods
beneath the counter

For you
I will be a doctor jew
and search
in all the garbage cans
for foreskins
to sew back again

For you
I will be a Dachau jew
and lie down in lime
with twisted limbs
and bloated pain
no mind can understand

The Only Tourist in Havana
Turns His Thoughts Homeward

Come, my brothers,
let us govern Canada,
let us find our serious heads,
let us dump asbestos on the White House,
let us make the French talk English,
    not only here but everywhere,
let us torture the Senate individually
    until they confess,
let us purge the New Party,
let us encourage the dark races
    so they'll be lenient
    when they take over,
let us make the CBC talk English,
let us all lean in one direction
    and float down
    to the coast of Florida,
let us have tourism,
let us flirt with the enemy,
let us smelt pig-iron in our back yards,
let us sell snow
    to under-developed nations
(Is it true one of our national leaders
    was a Roman Catholic?)
let us terrorize Alaska,
let us unite
    Church and State,
let us not take it lying down,
let us have two Governor Generals
    at the same time,
let us have another official language,
let us determine what it will be,
let us give a Canada Council Fellowship
    to the most original suggestion,
let us teach sex in the home
    to parents,

let us threaten to join the U.S.A.
    and pull out at the last moment,
my brothers, come,
our serious heads are waiting for us somewhere
    like Gladstone bags abandoned
    after a *coup d'état*,
let us put them on very quickly,
let us maintain a stony silence
    on the St. Lawrence Seaway.

Havana .
April 1961

Alexander Trocchi,
Public Junkie, Priez Pour Nous

Who is purer
    more simple than you?
Priests play poker with the burghers,
police in underwear
    leave Crime at the office,
our poets work bankers' hours
retire to wives and fame-reports.

The spike flashes in your blood
permanent as a silver lighthouse.

I'm apt to loaf
    in a coma of newspapers,
avoid the second-hand bodies
which cry to be catalogued.
I dream I'm
    a divine right Prime Minister,
I abandon plans for bloodshed in Canada.
I accept an O.B.E.

Under hard lights
with doctors' instruments
    you are at work
in the bathrooms of the city,
changing The Law.

I tend to get distracted
    by hydrogen bombs,
by Uncle's disapproval
    of my treachery
to the men's clothing industry.
I find myself
    believing public clocks,
taking advice
from the Dachau generation.

The spike hunts
constant as a compass.
    You smile like a Navajo
discovering American oil
on his official slum wilderness,
a surprise every half hour.

I'm afraid I sometimes forget
my lady's pretty little blond package
is an amateur time-bomb
set to fizzle in my middle-age.
    I forget the Ice Cap, the pea-minds,
the heaps of expensive teeth.

You don a false nose
line up twice for the Demerol dole;
you step out of a tourist group
shoot yourself on the steps of the White House,
you try to shoot the big arms
    of the Lincoln Memorial;
through a flaw in their lead houses
you spy on scientists,
    stumble on a cure for scabies;
you drop pamphlets from a stolen jet:
"The Truth about Junk";
you pirate a national TV commercial
shove your face against
    the window of the living-room
insist that healthy skin is grey.

A little blood in the sink
Red cog-wheels
    shaken from your arm
punctures inflamed
like a roadmap showing cities
over 10,000 pop.

53   Leonard Cohen

Your arms tell me
you have been reaching into the coke machine
for strawberries,
you have been humping the thorny crucifix
you have been piloting Mickey Mouse balloons
through the briar patch,
you have been digging for grins in the tooth-pile.

Bonnie Queen Alex Eludes Montreal Hounds
Famous Local Love Scribe Implicated

Your purity drives me to work.
I must get back to lust and microscopes,
experiments in embalming,
resume the census of my address book.

You leave behind you a fanatic
to answer RCMP questions.

For E. J. P.

I once believed a single line
    in a Chinese poem could change
        forever how blossoms fell
and that the moon itself climbed on
    the grief of concise weeping men
        to journey over cups of wine
I thought invasions were begun for crows
    to pick at a skeleton
        dynasties sown and spent
to serve the language of a fine lament
    I thought governors ended their lives
        as sweetly drunken monks
telling time by rain and candles
    instructed by an insect's pilgrimage
        across the page—all this
so one might send an exile's perfect letter
to an ancient home-town friend

I chose a lonely country
    broke from love
        scorned the fraternity of war
I polished my tongue against the pumice moon
    floated my soul in cherry wine
        a perfumed barge for Lords of Memory
to languish on to drink to whisper out
    their store of strength
        as if beyond the mist along the shore
their girls their power still obeyed
    like clocks wound for a thousand years
I waited until my tongue was sore

Brown petals wind like fire around my poems
    I aimed them at the stars but
        like rainbows they were bent
before they sawed the world in half
    Who can trace the canyoned paths
        cattle have carved out of time
wandering from meadowlands to feasts
    Layer after layer of autumn leaves
        are swept away
Something forgets us perfectly

I Met a Woman Long Ago

I met a woman long ago,
hair black as black can go.
Are you a teacher of the heart?
Soft she answered No.

I met a girl across the sea,
hair the gold that gold can be.
Are you a teacher of the heart?
Yes, but not for thee.

I knew a man who lost his mind
in some lost place I wished to find.
Follow me, he said,
but he walked behind.

I walked into a hospital
Where none was sick and none was well.
When at night the nurses left,
I could not walk at all.

55   Leonard Cohen

Not too slow, not too soon
morning came, then came noon.
Dinner time a scalpel blade
lay beside my spoon.

Some girls wander by mistake
into the mess that scalpels make.
Are you teachers of the heart?
We teach old hearts to break.

One day I woke up alone,
hospital and nurses gone.
Have I carved enough?
You are a bone.

I ate and ate and ate,
I didn't miss a plate.
How much do these suppers cost?
We'll take it out in hate.

I spent my hatred every place,
on every work, on every face.
Someone gave me wishes.
I wished for an embrace.

Several girls embraced me, then
I was embraced by men.
Is my passion perfect?
Do it once again.

I was handsome, I was strong,
I knew the words of every song.
Did my singing please you?
The words you sang were wrong.

Who are you whom I address?
Who takes down what I confess?
Are you a teacher of the heart?
A chorus answered Yes.

Teachers, are my lessons done
or must I learn another one?
They cried: Dear Sir or Madam,
Daughter, Son.

Suzanne Takes You Down

Suzanne takes you down
to her place near the river,
you can hear the boats go by
you can stay the night beside her.
And you know that she's half crazy
but that's why you want to be there
and she feeds you tea and oranges
that come all the way from China.
Just when you mean to tell her
that you have no gifts to give her,
she gets you on her wave-length
and she lets the river answer
that you've always been her lover.
    And you want to travel with her,
    you want to travel blind
    and you know that she can trust you
    because you've touched her perfect body
    with your mind.

Jesus was a sailor
when he walked upon the water
and he spent a long time watching
from a lonely wooden tower
and when he knew for certain
only drowning men could see him
he said All men will be sailors then
until the sea shall free them,
but he himself was broken
long before the sky would open,
forsaken, almost human,
he sank beneath your wisdom like a stone.
    And you want to travel with him,
    you want to travel blind
    and you think maybe you'll trust him
    because he touched your perfect body
    with his mind.

Suzanne takes your hand
and she leads you to the river,
she is wearing rags and feathers
from Salvation Army counters.
The sun pours down like honey
on our lady of the harbour
as she shows you where to look
among the garbage and the flowers,
there are heroes in the seaweed
there are children in the morning,
they are leaning out for love
they will lean that way forever
while Suzanne she holds the mirror.
> And you want to travel with her
> and you want to travel blind
> and you're sure that she can find you
> because she's touched her perfect body
> with her mind.

I Believe You Heard Your Master Sing

I believe you heard your master sing
while I lay sick in bed
I believe he told you everything
I keep locked in my head
Your master took you traveling
at least that's what you said
O love did you come back to bring
your prisoner wine and bread

You met him at some temple where
they take your clothes at the door
He was just a numberless man of a pair
who has just come back from the war
You wrap his quiet face in your hair
and he hands you the apple core
and he touches your mouth now so suddenly bare
of the kisses you had on before

He gave you a German shepherd to walk
with a collar of leather and nails
He never once made you explain or talk
about all of the little details
such as who had a worm and who had a rock
and who had you through the mails
Your love is a secret all over the block
and it never stops when he fails

He took you on his air-o-plane
which he flew without any hands
and you cruised above the ribbons of rain
that drove the crowd from the stands
Then he killed the lights on a lonely lane
where an ape with angel glands
erased the final wisps of pain
with the music of rubber bands

And now I hear your master sing
You pray for him to come
His body is a golden string
that your body is hanging from
His body is a golden string
My body is growing numb
O love I hear your master sing
Your shirt is all undone

Will you kneel beside the bed
we polished long ago
before your master chose instead
to make my bed of snow
Your hair is wild your knuckles red
and you're speaking much too low
I can't make out what your master said
before he made you go

I think you're playing far too rough
For a lady who's been to the moon
I've lain by the window long enough
(you get used to an empty room)
Your love is some dust in an old man's cuff
who is tapping his foot to a tune
and your thighs are a ruin and you want too much
Let's say you came back too soon

I loved your master perfectly
I taught him all he knew
He was starving in a mystery
like a man who is sure what is true
I sent you to him with my guarantee
I could teach him something new
I taught him how you would long for me
No matter what he said no matter what you do

George Bowering

Inside the Tulip

Inside the tulip
we make love
on closer look
seeing faint green lines, new

Let me share this flower
with you, kiss you
press my tongue on pollen
against the roof of my mouth

Look at me long enough
and I will be a flower
or wet blackberries dangling
from a dripping bush

Let me share you
with this flower, look
at anything long enough
and it is water

on a leaf, a petal
where we lie, bare legs together

The Grass

I must tell you
of the brown grass
that has twenty times
this year, appeared
from under the
melting snow, reared
its version of spring
like a sea lion coming
out of water, a-dazzle
in the sun, this
brave grass the sun
will only burn again
returning like a tiny
season.

The Swing

Renoir's people
        seem to stand
                on a forest floor
of blossoms.

                The girl on the swing
could be fifteen, her dress
        of new flowers.

                        She leans coyly
or thoughtfully away
        from the two men
                with straw hats.

They are artists
        on a Sunday afternoon
                warm in loose clothing,

some kind of wonder
        for the child who
                makes the fourth figure.

She is clasping her empty hands
        in front of her, her head up,
                her eyes the only ones
                        looking outward.

Esta Muy Caliente

On the highway
near San Juan del Río
we had to stop the car
for a funeral.

The whole town it was
a hundred people or
two hundred
walking slowly along the highway

toward th yellow domed church
on the top of the hill
and we pulled into the shade
of a shaggy tree.

I turned off the engine
and we heard their music
a screeching saxophone
and high broken noted trumpet

alone and sad in the hot afternoon
as they walked slow like sheep
the women with black shawls
the men in flappy trousers.

Every five minutes the men
threw cherry bombs into the air
behind them: loud gun shots
blasting the afternoon

then the saxophone: tin music
odd tortured jazz
in that mysterious Indian Christian march
up the hill: bearing a coffin to the priest.

It was a small coffin
on the shoulder of one man in front
          the father we thought
the cherry bombs were like violence

against us: but we were stopped.
An old rattling truck
nosed thru them: and they closed
together again behind it
                              ignoring us.

I walked away from the road
in among the bushes and prickly pear
looking for scorpions on the hot sand
and took a leak beside a thin horse.

An hour later the road was clear
and as I got in the car
a man on a donkey came by
a San Juan lonely in the mountains man.

Good afternoon, I said.
Good afternoon, he said, it is very hot.
Yes it is, I said, especially for us.
It is very hot for us too, he said.

A Sudden Measure

This sudden snow:
    immediately
the prairie is!

Those houses are:
    dark
under roofs of snow –

That hill up to the cloud is:
    marked
by snow creeks down to town –

This footpath is:
    a bare line
across white field –

    This woman appears
    thru drift of snow:

a red coat.

The Blue

The Bow River
was blue today,
the sky,
the Rockies somewhere

that is, the mud
has sunk,
the ice
disappeared sometime.

I would do that,
disappear sometime
like a blue river
on the prairie.

Indian Summer

The yellow trees
along the river

are dying I said
they are in
their moment of life
you said.

The Indians I think
are dead, you cant
immortalize them, a
leaf presst between
pages becomes a
page.

In a month
the river will move

beneath ice, moving
as it always does
south. We will
believe it as we

will no longer see
those yellow borders
of the river.

Footprints, Fenceposts

On the prairie
with fresh snow
one set of footprints
is a line to
some distance.

Because it is
morning, there is
snow also on top
of every fence post.

65   George Bowering

culling specks of straw,
        from tweed suit
        pantleg over knee
        stretching to expose
        seam
        encrusted with soil
        of other climes, alas

Forget

We forget those
apartment blocks
were made step-
by-step by
human hands.

The glue on this
envelope too
it tastes like
a pear.

Thru

She says it makes her mad
I wake her up
laughing in my sleep.

I dont remember that happiness
wrapt with her & the sheets,
& if it is the edge of

what? where is that place,
maybe for ease we call it eternity,
what was funny there?

Dont wake the sleep-
walker they say, how about
the man giggling with his eyes closed?

He may be left in the place
we court so solemnly
in our poems – he may

have been laughing
to enrich his courage, faced
with unspeakable horror.

Or one time I will
catch myself laughing among friends,
& a glimpse of it,

in the moment their faces
melt away, that instant's
springtime, the monster

under the grass, that I return to,
the mystery best forgotten
in the springtime of waking

to the alarm, the alarm.

Particulars On The Picture Cards

I dont care what your later calculations show,
I like to be as you first figured
king of swords,

            being to begin with
saggitarius, desert-born, sentimental
about the forties,

            I mean my childhood horn
was radio Lester Young, on KGO, not being able
to pick up a Canadian station.

I burn my hair every time
I light a cigar on the gas burner, that shows
a certain carelessness, something I have
memories of being accused of, by
my mother,

            never by anyone since. My early
direction having some value to it,
I imagine.

        The king of swords
has some of that by virtue of his strength,
but some of the other, by reason
of his well-gathered wisdom, that being
what I am accused of lately.

The well I go to never threatens
to drown my face,
                       & the darkness there
affords no reflection to fear or fall to.
I have friends like that,
                           but I no longer
envy them. I indulge my secret longing
for two decades ago, & listen
to the horn that's been blowing since then.

The Envies

I watcht as the flung screen door
slammed across our kitten's throat
& my father took it to the garage
to do what I didnt see
where I was still
in the porch.

I watcht as one brother fell
breaking his head on a rock
in the newly dug foundation & my father
took him to the hospital
& he later shared my bedroom,
a cast around his skull.

I sat & watcht as the other
opened the back door of the moving car
to step out over the pavement
& my father reacht back from the wheel
to pull him in.

& now I'm under that history
stored behind the eyes
where all household pets are forgotten
& I have contrived to
get my brothers out of a prairie jail.

They are both taller than I,
& we come together across our decade,
across the envies looking at one another,
men in a place
where smaller things die early.

On Quadra Island

There are places you come from
I must remember,

that is our child still in me
will come from there.

So you show me Granite Bay
& I see some dark water,

two buildings, one a float house
& an empty post office.

You attest that the bay
was ringed by houses

& you, one of two children there
held the crazed loggers in thrall.

It is deserted now, rusht
into your eyes I explore

poking among pebbles at low tide,
hardly disturbing the small crabs

I suddenly see all around us.

John Newlove

Black Night Window

Black night window –
rain running down
the fogged glass,

a blanched leaf
hanging outside
on a dead twig,

the moon dead,
the wind dying
in the trees,

in this valley,
in this recession.

Everyone

Everyone is so
lonely in this
country that
it's necessary
to be fantastic –

a crow flew over
my grave today,
no goose stepping
pompously along,

but a crow,
black as life,
raucously calling
to no one –

struggling image:
necessary
to be fantastic
almost to lie,

but incorrect,
not cautious enough,
though not evil
actively: it does not

have the diminishing
virtue of evilness
(a locked sea-monster
with half the

dangerous coils
waving above
the grey water),
for the tourists,
glistening crows.

Lady, Lady

Lady, lady, I cannot lie,
I didn't cut down your cherry tree.

It was another man, in another season,
for the same reason.

I eat the stone and not the flesh,
it is the bare bone of desire I want,

something you would throw a dog,
or me, though I insult by saying so.

God knows it is not said
of your body, that it is like

a bone thrown to a dog,
or that I would throw it away, which

moment to moment I cannot remember
under those baggy clothes you wear –

which, if I love and tell,
I love well.

The Original Peg-leg

(*An Approach to Occupational Therapy*, Second Edition, 1960,
by Mary S. Jones, Butterworth, London)

They experimented, using an old-fashioned
wooden shoe-tree that fitted

the patient's shoe, says the book;
a beech-bar two inches square

was employed instead of a broomstick;
the shoe-tree was drilled through

at what would have been the ankle-joint
and this hole bushed with brass tubing

for a neat turn; using calipers
and the ordinary carpentry instruments,

they attached a complicated mass
of angle-irons, cup-hooks and six inch

iron springs. The patient, soon active,
discarded sticks and similar supports

and even played cricket, bowling and batting,
a vigorous young man lacking one leg,

a spare spring kept in his pocket
since twice he had broken one in his games,

leaping to catch the hard-hit ball
and landing awkwardly, never forgetting
the original shock of it all.

73   John Newlove

The Double-Headed Snake

Not to lose the feel of the mountains
while still retaining the prairies
is a difficult thing. What's lovely
is whatever makes the adrenalin run;
therefore I count terror and fear among
the greatest beauty. The greatest
beauty is to be alive, forgetting nothing,
although remembrance hurts
like a foolish act, is a foolish act.

Beauty's whatever
makes the adrenalin run. Fear
in the mountains at night-time's
not tenuous, it is not the cold
that makes me shiver, civilized man,
white, I remember
the stories of the Indians,
Sis-i-utl, the double-headed snake.

Beauty's what makes
the adrenalin run. Fear at night
on the level plains, with no horizon
and the stars too bright, wind bitter
even in June, in winter
the snow harsh and blowing,
is what makes me
shiver, not the cold air alone.

And one beauty cancels another. The plains
seem secure and comfortable
at Crow's Nest Pass; in Saskatchewan
the mountains are comforting
to think of; among
the eastwardly diminishing hills
both the flatland and the ridge
seem easy to endure.

As one beauty
cancels another, remembrance
is a foolish act, a double-headed snake
striking in both directions, but I
remember plains and mountains, places
I come from, places I adhere and live in.

Brass Box. Spring. Time.

I have a brass box for cigarettes and
two pair of shoes and

numerous shirts – red and white
checks, blue stripes, black stripes,

pale yellow stripes – I have white paper
and carbon paper to make a good impression,

and two wallets but no money,

I have red pencils and blue pencils and
green pencils and I have jars
of various sizes to keep them in

and a pot to catch the ceiling's rain and
clay ashtrays and, and, and –

I have a brass box for cigarettes,
when I have cigarettes.

When I Heard of the Friend's Death

When I heard of the friend's death in the mechanized city,
who was so clever, so young, so pleasant, I was ashamed

to be alive, all my faults in me, and him spoiled,
dirty and unreasonable at the accident's will.

Just so it is horrible to think of my father on his dead back
in the box, packed under dirt, his handsome face

falling apart. How curiously we deceive ourselves.

There is no consolation to be had anywhere for this.
There is always so much more to be said than can be said.

75   John Newloye

A Film of Lhasa

In the film shot by one of their
brethren the monks move with ease
across an overexposed landscape.
Dalai Lama is going to three monas-
teries to pass his exams. It is the first
time I have seen a man almost a god
moving.

The scattered bushes are light
green on white soil, the garments of
the lesser men have been washed
many times.

All move slowly, chatting – no
urgency when a man becomes a god
or part of a god. It is ordained, what
will happen; the perfect moments
will be found. And exalted the ordi-
nances!

An emperor of Rome smiling on
the deathbed sardonically made a
joke of his impending divinity. Dalai
Lama does not die; he smiles, moving
back and forth, he questions the ex-
aminers and claps his hands like a
small delighted boy.

Samuel Hearne in Wintertime

1. In this cold room
   I remember the smell of manure
   on men's heavy clothes as good,
   the smell of horses.

   It is a romantic world
   to readers of journeys
   to the Northern Ocean –

   especially if their houses are heated
   to some degree, Samuel.

Hearne, your camp must have smelled
like hell whenever you settled down
for a few days of rest and journal-work:

hell smeared with human manure,
hell half-full of raw hides,
hell of sweat, Indians, stale fat,
meat-hell, fear-hell, hell of cold.

2. One child is back from the doctor's while
the other one wanders about in dirty pants
and I think of Samuel Hearne and the land –

puffy children coughing as I think,
crying, sick-faced,
vomit stirring in grey blankets
from room to room.

It is Christmastime –
the cold flesh shines.
No praise in merely enduring.

3. Samuel Hearne did more
in the land (like all the rest

full of rocks and hilly country,
many very extensive tracts of land,
tittimeg, pike and barble,

and the islands:
the islands, many
of them abound

as well as the main
land does
with dwarf woods.

chiefly pine
in some parts intermixed
with larch and birch) than endure.

The Indians killed twelve deer.
It was impossible to describe
the intenseness of the cold.

4. And, Samuel Hearne,
   I have almost begun to talk

   as if you wanted to be
   gallant, as if you went
   through that land for a book –

   as if you were not SAM, wanting
   to know, to do a job.

5. There was that Eskimo girl
   at Bloody Falls, at your feet

   Samuel Hearne, with two spears in her,
   you helpless before your helpers,

   and she twisted about them like
   an eel, dying, never to know.

The Pride

I

The image/ the pawnees
in their earth-lodge villages,
the clear image
of teton sioux, wild
fickle people the chronicler says

the crazy dogs, men
tethered with leather dog-thongs
to a stake, fighting until dead,

image: arikaras
with traded spanish sabre blades
mounted on the long
heavy buffalo lances,
riding the sioux
down, the centaurs, the horsemen
scouring the level plains
in war or hunt
until smallpox got them,
4,000 warriors,

image – of a desolate country,
a long way between fires,
unfound lakes, mirages, cold rocks,
and lone men going through it,
cree with good guns
creating terror in athabaska
among the inhabitants, frightened
stone-age people, "so that
they fled at the mere sight
of a strange smoke miles away."

II

This western country crammed
with the ghosts of indians,
haunting the coastal stones and shores,
the forested pacific islands,
mountains, hills and plains:

beside the ocean ethlinga,
man in the moon, empties
his bucket, on
a sign from Spirit
of the Wind ethlinga
empties his bucket, refreshing
the earth, and it rains
on the white cities;

that black joker, broken-
jawed raven, most prominent
among haida and tsimshyan tribes,
is in the kwakiut!
dance masks too –
it was he who brought fire,
food and water to man,
the trickster;

and thunderbird hilunga,
little thought of
by haida for lack of thunderstorms
in their district, goes
by many names, exquisite disguises
carved in the painted wood,

he is nootka tootooch, the wings
causing thunder and the tongue
or flashing eyes engendering
rabid white lightning,
whose food was whales,
called kwunusela by the kwakiutl,
it was he who laid down the house-logs
for the people at Place
Where Kwunusela Alighted;

in full force and virtue
and terror of the law, eagle –
he is authority, the sun
assumed his form once,
the sun which used to be
a flicker's egg, success-
fully transformed;

and malevolence comes to the land,
the wild woman of the woods;
grinning, she wears
a hummingbird in her hair,
d'sonoqua, the furious one –

they are all ready
to be found, the legends
and the people, or
all their ghosts and memories,
whatever is strong enough
to be remembered.

III

But what image, bewildered
son of all men
under the hot sun,
do you worship,
what completeness
do you hope to have
from these tales,
a half-understood massiveness, mirage,
in men's minds – what
is your purpose;

with what force
will you proceed
along a line
neither straight nor short,
whose future
you cannot know
or result foretell,
whose meaning is still
obscured as the incidents
occur and accumulate?

IV

The country moves on;
there are orchards in the interior,
the mountain passes
are broken, the foothills
covered with cattle and fences,
and the fading hills covered;

but the plains are bare,
not barren, easy
for me to love their people,
for me to love their people
without selection.

V

In 1787, the old cree saukamappee,
aged 75 or thereabout, speaking then
of things that had happened when he was 16,
just a man, told david thompson,
of the raids the shoshonis,
the snakes, had made on the westward-
reaching peigan, of their war-parties
sometimes sent 10 days journey to enemy camps,
the men all afoot in battle array for
the encounter, crouching
behind their giant shields;
the peigan armed with guns
drove these snakes out of the plains,
the plains where their strength had been,
where they had been settled since living
memory (though nothing is remembered
beyond a grandfather's time),
to the west of the rockies;

these people moved without rest,
backward and forward with the wind,
the seasons, the game, great herds,
in hunger and abundance –

in summer and in the bloody fall
they gathered on the killing grounds,
fat and shining with fat, amused
with the luxuries of war and death,

relieved from the steam of knowledge,
consoled by the stream of blood
and steam rising from the fresh hides
and tired horses, wheeling in their pride
on the sweating horses, their pride.

VI

Those are all stories;
the pride, the grand poem
of our land, of the earth itself,
will come, welcome, and
sought for, and found,
in a line of running verse,
sweating, our pride;

we seize on
what has happened before,
one line only
will be enough,
a single line and
then the sunlit brilliant image suddenly floods us
with understanding, shocks our
attentions, and all desire
stops, stands alone;

we stand alone,
we are no longer lonely
but have roots,
and the rooted words
recur in the mind, mirror, so that
we dwell on nothing else, in nothing else,
touched, repeating them,
at home freely
at last, in amazement;

"the unyielding phrase
in tune with the epoch,"
the thing made up
of our desires,
not of its words, not only
of them, but of something else,
as well, that which we desire
so ardently, that which
will not come when
it is summoned alone,
but grows in us
and idles about and hides
until the moment is due –

the knowledge of
our origins, and where
we are in truth,
whose land this is
and is to be.

VII

The unyielding phrase:
when the moment is due, then
it springs upon us
out of our own mouths,
unconsidered, overwhelming
in its knowledge, complete –

not this handful
of fragments, as the indians
are not composed of
the romantic stories
about them, or of the stories
they tell only, but
still ride the soil
in us, dry bones a part
of the dust in our eyes,
needed and troubling
in the glare, in
our breath, in our
ears, in our mouths,
in our bodies entire, in our minds, until at
last we become them

in our desires, our desires,
mirages, mirrors, that are theirs, hard-
riding desires, and they
become our true forbears, moulded
by the same wind or rain,
and in this land we
are their people, come
back to life again.

Everywhere I Go

What are people talking about. Everywhere I go they whisper.

They stick their eyes at me, right at the base of the breastbone,
when I'm not looking.

The breastbone seems flat, pointed like a dagger to the top of my
stomach.

O, my stomach, my stomach . . . when the knife rips you open it will
find coffee and four strips of bacon, pieces of chewed beard and a
handwritten note saying I have left town forever again.

Margaret Atwood

This is a Photograph of Me

It was taken some time ago.
At first it seems to be
a smeared
print: blurred lines and grey flecks
blended with the paper;

then, as you scan
it, you see in the left-hand corner
a thing that is like a branch: part of a tree
(balsam or spruce) emerging
and, to the right, halfway up
what ought to be a gentle
slope, a small frame house.

In the background there is a lake,
and beyond that, some low hills.

(The photograph was taken
the day after I drowned.

I am in the lake, in the center
of the picture, just under the surface.

It is difficult to say where
precisely, or to say
how large or small I am:
the effect of water
on light is a distortion

but if you look long enough,
eventually
you will be able to see me.)

After The Flood, We

We must be the only ones
left, in the mist that has risen
everywhere as well
as in these woods

I walk across the bridge
towards the safety of high ground
(the tops of the trees are like islands)

gathering the sunken
bones of the drowned mothers
(hard and round in my hands)
while the white mist washes
around my legs like water;

fish must be swimming
down in the forest beneath us,
like birds, from tree to tree
and a mile away
the city, wide and silent,
is lying lost, far undersea.

You saunter beside me, talking
of the beauty of the morning,
not even knowing
that there has been a flood,

tossing small pebbles
at random over your shoulder
into the deep thick air,

not hearing the first stumbling
footsteps of the almost-born
coming (slowly) behind us,
not seeing
the almost-human
brutal faces forming
(slowly)
out of stone.

On The Streets, Love

On the streets
love
these days
is a matter for
either scavengers
(turning death to life) or
(turning life
to death) for predators

(The billboard lady
with her white enamel
teeth and red
enamel claws, is after

        the men
        when they pass her
        never guess they have brought her
        to life, or that her
        body's made of cardboard, or in her
        veins flows the drained
        blood of their desire)
(Look, the grey man
his footsteps soft
as flan-
nel, glides from his poster

        and the voracious women, seeing
        him so trim,
        edges clear as cut paper
        eyes clean
        and sharp as lettering,
        want to own him
        . . . are you dead? are you dead?
        they say, hoping . . .)

Love, what are we to do
on the streets these days
and how am I
to know that you
and how are you to know
that I, that

we are not parts of those
people, scraps glued together
waiting for a chance
to come to life

(One day
I'll touch the warm
flesh of your throat, and hear
a faint crackle of paper

or you, who think
that you can read my mind
from the inside out, will taste the
black ink on my tongue, and find
the fine print written
just beneath my skin.)

Journey To the Interior

There are similarities
I notice: that the hills
which the eyes make flat as a wall, welded
together, open as I move
to let me through; become
endless as prairies; that the trees
grow spindly, have their roots
often in swamps; that this is a poor country;
that a cliff is not known
as rough except by hand, and is
therefore inaccessible. Mostly
that travel is not the easy going
from point to point, a dotted
line on a map, location
plotted on a square surface
but that I move surrounded by a tangle
of branches, a net of air and alternate
light and dark, at all times;
that there are no destinations
apart from this.

There are differences
of course: the lack of reliable charts;
more important, the distraction of small details:
your shoe among the brambles under the chair
where it shouldn't be; lucent
white mushrooms and a paring knife
on the kitchen table; a sentence
crossing my path, sodden as a fallen log
I'm sure I passed yesterday

                              (have I been

walking in circles again?)

but mostly the danger:
many have been here, but only
some have returned safely.
A compass is useless; also
trying to take directions
from the movements of the sun,
which are erratic;
and words here are as pointless
as calling in a vacant
wilderness.

                    Whatever I do I must
keep my head. I know
it is easier for me to lose my way
forever here, than in other landscapes

A Place: Fragments

i)

Here on the rim, cringing
under the cracked whip of winter
we live
in houses of ice,
but not because we want to:
in order to survive
we make what we can and have to
with what we have.

ii)

Old woman I visited once
out of my way
in a little-visited province:

89   Margaret Atwood

she had a neat
house, a clean parlour
though obsolete and poor:

a cushion with a fringe;
glass animals arranged
across the mantlepiece (a swan, a horse,
a bull); a mirror;
a teacup sent from Scotland;
several heraldic spoons;
a lamp; and in the center
of the table, a paperweight:
hollow glass globe
filled with water, and
a house, a man, a snowstorm.

The room was as
dustless as possible
and free of spiders.
                              I
stood in the door-
way, at the fulcrum where

this trivial but
stringent inner order
held its delicate balance
with the random scattering or
clogged merging of
things: ditch by the road; dried
reeds in the wind; flat
wet bush, grey sky
sweeping away outside.

iii)

The cities are only outposts.

Watch that man
 walking on cement as though on snowshoes:
senses the road
a muskeg, loose mat of roots and brown
vegetable decay
or crust of ice that
easily might break and
slush or water under
suck him down.

The land flows like a
sluggish current.

The mountains eddy slowly towards the sea.

iv)

The people who come here also
flow: their bodies becoming
nebulous, diffused, quietly
spreading out into the air across
these interstellar sidewalks

v)

This is what it must be
like in outer space
where the stars are pasted flat
against the total
black of the expanding
eye, fly-
specks of burning dust

vi)

There is no center;
the centers
travel with us unseen
like our shadows
on a day when there is no sun.

We must move back:
there are too many foregrounds.

Now, clutter of twigs
across our eyes, tatter
of birds at the eye's edge; the straggle
of dead treetrunks; patch
of lichen
and in love, tangle
of limbs and fingers, the texture
of pores and lines on the skin.

An other sense tugs at us:
we have lost something,
some key to these things
which must be writings
and are locked against us
or perhaps (like a potential
mine, unknown vein
of metal in the rock)
something not lost or hidden
but just not found yet

that informs, holds together
this confusion, this largeness
and dissolving:

not above or behind
or within it, but one
with it: an

identity:
something too huge and simple
for us to see.

The animals in that country

In that country the animals
have the faces of people:

the ceremonia!
cats possessing the streets

the fox run
politely to earth, the huntsmen
standing around him, fixed
in their tapestry of manners

the bull, embroidered
with blood and given
an elegant death, trumpets, his name
stamped on him, heraldic brand
because

(when he rolled
on the sand, sword in his heart, the teeth
in his blue mouth were human)

he is really a man

even the wolves, holding resonant
conversations in their
forests thickened with legend.

> In this country the animals
> have the faces of
> animals.
>
> Their eyes
> flash once in car headlights
> and are gone.
>
> Their deaths are not elegant.
>
> They have the faces of
> no-one.

The Landlady

This is the lair of the landlady.

She is
a raw voice
loose in the rooms beneath me,

the continuous henyard
squabble going on below
thought in this house like
the bicker of blood through the head.

She is everywhere, intrusive as the smells
that bulge in under my doorsill;
she presides over my
meagre eating, generates
the light for eyestrain.

From her I rent my time:
she slams
my days like doors.
Nothing is mine

and when I dream images
of daring escapes through the snow
I find myself walking
always over a vast face
which is the land-
lady's, and wake up shouting.

She is a bulk, a knot
swollen in space. Though I have tried
to find some way around
her, my senses
are cluttered by perception
and can't see through her.

She stands there, a raucous fact
blocking my way:
immutable, a slab
of what is real,

solid as bacon.

At the tourist centre in Boston

There is my country under glass,
a white relief –
map with red dots for the cities,
reduced to the size of a wall

and beside it 10 blownup snapshots
one for each province,
in purple-browns and odd reds
the green of the trees dulled;
all blues however
of an assertive purity.

Mountains and lakes and more lakes
(though Quebec is a restaurant and Ontario the empty
interior of the parliament buildings),
with nobody climbing the trails and hauling out
the fish and splashing in the water

but arrangements of grinning tourists –
look here, Saskatchewan
is a flat lake, some convenient rocks
where two children pose with a father
and the mother is cooking something
in immaculate slacks by a smokeless fire,
her teeth white as detergent.

Whose dream is this, I would like to know:
is this a manufactured
hallucination, a cynical fiction, a lure
for export only?

I seem to remember people,
at least in the cities, also slush,
machines and assorted garbage. Perhaps
that was my private mirage

which will just evaporate
when I go back. Or the citizens will be gone,
run off to the peculiarly –
green forests
to wait among the brownish mountains
for the platoons of tourists
and plan their odd red massacres.

Unsuspecting
window lady, I ask you:

Do you see nothing
watching you from under the water?

Was the sky ever that blue?

Who really lives there?

A night in the Royal Ontario Museum

Who locked me

into this crazed man-made
stone brain
              where the weathered
totempole jabs a blunt
finger at the byzantine
mosaic dome

Under that ornate
golden cranium I wander
among fragments of gods, tarnished
coins, embalmed gestures
chronologically arranged,
looking for the EXIT sign

but in spite of the diagrams
at every corner, labelled
in red: YOU ARE HERE
the labyrinth holds me,

turning me around
the cafeteria, the washrooms,
a spiral through marble
Greece and Rome, the bronze
horses of China

then past the carved masks, wood and fur
to where 5 plaster Indians
in a glass case
squat near a dusty fire

and further, confronting me
with a skeleton child, preserved
in the desert air, curled
beside a clay pot and a few beads.

I say I am far
enough,   stop here   please
no more

but the perverse museum, corridor
by corridor, an idiot
voice jogged by a pushed
button, repeats its memories

and I am dragged to the mind's
deadend, the roar of the bone-
yard, I am lost
among the mastodons
and beyond: a fossil
shell, then

samples of rocks
and minerals, even the thundering
tusks dwindling to pin-
points in the stellar
fluorescent-lighted
wastes of geology

The gods avoid revealing themselves

The figures of the gods
I saw, bright blue, bright
green in the torchfire, standing
on grave colossal feet
with metal feathers and hooked
oracular beaks and human bodies
polished, reflecting but also
giving out their own light.

Before I could ask anything
they rose and wheeled
and wheeling spent their shiny
energy: descended into
a granite circle of godbones and shed
feathers closed in symmetry
that through long minutes and without answer
dissolved to sand in the background.

After that I was being driven
over a familiar shore
highway between the sea
and the wooded cliffs. Above the water
the sun smoked golden
and the gulls floated and called.
The figures of the gods
were everywhere, but invisible.

Beside me at the wheel was someone
who might have been
bright green, bright blue,
who would not let himself be seen.

Backdrop addresses cowboy

Starspangled cowboy
sauntering out of the almost-
silly West, on your face
a porcelain grin,
tugging a papier-mâché cactus
on wheels behind you with a string.

you are innocent as a bathtub
full of bullets.

Your righteous eyes, your laconic
trigger-fingers
people the streets with villains:
as you move, the air in front of you
blossoms with targets

and you leave behind you a heroic
trail of desolation:
beer bottles
slaughtered by the side
of the road, bird-
skulls bleaching in the sunset.

I ought to be watching
from behind a cliff or a cardboard storefront
when the shooting starts, hands clasped
in admiration,

but I am elsewhere.

Then what about me

what about the I
confronting you on that border
you are always trying to cross?

I am the horizon
you ride towards, the thing you can never lasso

I am also what surrounds you:
my brain
scattered with you
tincans, bones, empty shells,
the litter of your invasions.

I am the space you desecrate
as you pass through.

Further Arrivals

After we had crossed the long illness
that was the ocean, we sailed up-river

On the first island
the immigrants threw off their clothes
and danced like sandflies

We left behind one by one
the cities rotting with cholera,
one by one our civilized
distinctions

and entered a large darkness.

It was our own
ignorance we entered.

I have not come out yet

My brain gropes nervous
tentacles in the night, sends out
fears hairy as bears,
demands lamps; or waiting

for my shadowy husband, hears
malice in the trees' whispers.

I need wolf's eyes to see
the truth.

I refuse to look in a mirror.

Whether the wilderness is
real or not
depends on who lives there.

Departure From the Bush

I, who had been erased
by fire, was crept in
upon by green
                (how
lucid a season)

                In time the animals
arrived to inhabit me,

first one
  by one, stealthily
(their habitual traces
burnt); then
having marked new boundaries
returning, more
confident, year
by year, two
by two

but restless: I was not ready
altogether to be moved into

They could tell I was
too heavy: I might
capsize;

I was frightened
by their eyes (green or
amber) glowing out from inside me

I was not completed; at night
I could not see without lanterns.

He wrote, We are leaving. I said
I have no clothes
left I can wear

The snow came. The sleigh was a relief;
its track lengthened behind,
pushing me towards the city

and rounding the first hill, I was
(instantaneous)
unlived in: they had gone.

There was something they almost taught me
I came away not having learned.

Girl and Horse, 1928

You are younger than I am, you are
someone I never knew, you stand
under a tree, your face half-shadowed,
holding the horse by its bridle.

Why do you smile? Can't you
see the apple blossoms falling around
you, snow, sun, snow, listen, the tree
dries and is being burnt, the wind

is bending your body, your face
ripples like water   where did you go
But no, you stand there exactly
the same, you can't hear me, forty

years ago you were caught by light
and fixed in that secret
place where we live, where we believe
nothing can change, grow older.

(On the other side
of the picture, the instant
is over, the shadow
of the tree has moved.   You wave,

then turn and ride
out of sight through the vanished
orchard, still smiling
as though you do not notice)

Procedures for Underground

(Northwest Coast)

The country beneath
the earth has a green sun
and the rivers flow backwards;

the trees and rocks are the same
as they are here, but shifted.
Those who live there are always hungry;

from them you can learn
wisdom and great power,
if you can descend and return safely.

You must look for tunnels, animal
burrows or the cave in the sea
guarded by the stone man;

when you are down you will find
those who were once your friends
but they will be changed and dangerous.

Resist them, be careful
never to eat their food.
Afterwards, if you live, you will be able

to see them when they prowl as winds,
as thin sounds in our village. You will
tell us their names, what they want, who

has made them angry by forgetting them.
For this gift, as for all gifts, you must
suffer: those from the underland

will be always with you, whispering their
complaints, beckoning you
back down; while among us here

you will walk wrapped in an invisible
cloak. Few will seek your help
with love, none without fear.

Younger Sister, Going Swimming

(Northern Quebec)

Beside this lake
where there are no other people

my sister in bathing suit continues
her short desolate
parade to the end of the dock;

against the boards
her feet make sad statements
she thinks no one can hear;

(I sit in a deckchair
not counting, invisible;
the sun wavers on
this page as on a pool.)

She moves the raft out
past the sandy point;
no one comes by in a motorboat.

She would like to fill the lake
with other swimmers, with answers.
She calls her name. The sun encloses
rocks, trees, her feet in the water, the circling
bays and hills as before.

She poises, raises her arms
as though signalling, then disappears.
The lake heals itself quietly
of the wound left by the diver.
The air quakes and is still.

(Under my hand the paper
closes over these
marks I am making on it.

The words ripple, subside,
move outwards toward the shore.)

They eat out

In restaurants we argue
over which of us will pay for your funeral

though the real question is
whether or not I will make you immortal.

At the moment only I
can do it and so

I raise the magic fork
over the plate of beef fried rice

and plunge it into your heart.
There is a faint pop, a sizzle

and through your own split head
you rise up glowing;

the ceiling opens
a voice sings Love Is A Many

Splendoured Thing
you hang suspended above the city

in blue tights and a red cape,
your eyes flashing in unison.

The other diners regard you
some with awe, some only with boredom:

they cannot decide if you are a new weapon
or only a new advertisement.

As for me, I continue eating;
I liked you better the way you were,
but you were always ambitious.

After the agony in the guest
bedroom, you lying by the
overturned bed
your face uplifted, neck propped
against the windowsill, my arm
under you, cold moon
shining down through the window

wine mist rising
around you, an almost-
visible halo

You say, Do you
love me, do you love me

I answer you:
I stretch your arms out
one to either side,
your head slumps forward.

Later I take you home
in a taxi, and you
are sick in the bathtub.

bill bissett

this tree of night has stood
in the town here for 30 years
the bronze maiden smiled
as a relic to imagination
i have not yet all the facts

the comfort was mystery
and what we brought ourselves

this painting I do now is dull
i can't bring myself to believe
i haven't done it before
from the impression of the one previous

in all our minds
there are all answers
but not all questions

he had a crucifix above his bed
on the wall we calld him anglo-catholic
what did he do   he joind th air-force
came back to marry my best frien's sister
she has red hair to have babies and
go hungry in Toronto clerking
and he was beautiful

into this ready-made cavity i put
the blue stroke next this olive green
wham bang thank u maam
vanity al is vanity strange that place
where yu hate to get paint on yur hands
to have made an image

this paint is practically frozen
this date square sure tastes good

moon cloud wash away see how
the silver birch sings
to herself in the garden

water eyes

we are such
children we lean

on each other
in the wind

storm, there is no
rest for days

th law makes us
sin

comfort, there is no
clear shore for th head

dancing, we see
each other again

i told them i
wasint nice

sleep, days on end
of interrupted dream

what right
have we to death, it
is just what takes
place

    over life
we call it every day
when it is not there,

adore the stricken muscul
as a prelude to th last
gasp our lungs take in

of air

s
sometimes
circular
is
yellow in
ourselves

s in the feet
how we move
closer always
into our
origins

is flat
on the eye
a penny
madness

business,
is deeply
in cycle

moon, hot
of pupil
cold, lash
blink, into
our stride

s
sometimes
oval, our
dreams
enclosd

pictures
we see, of
the tides

lost yr way

dont bargain with love
  th babies are deep
  in th forest

dont make sense of it
    yu are such sense
      as appears

wait out th rain
  let th words
    fall away

lighten yr burden
  th babies will
  cum to yu with candy
  stories

        before yu go ovr
yr depth, cud they be
   wrong

song composed just after th alarm clock
before going to social assistance

who was that in th red boat
riding down sugar lane

who was that in th red boat
riding down sugar lane

who did yu see in th red boat
riding down sugar lane

who cud yu hear in th red boat
never to hear again

who cud yu hear in th red boat
never to hear again

eat makes th heart's window

or Martina

Onyx, th figure of her gaze
arries thruout long fields of snow
lowing, orange, th nails touching
   our wish clothd

   what metal holds, as th golden ring

aven, her hair, longer than ever is green
h sweet suckling tastes, meat to my brain
eaches, as th rainbow grows to circul
n th water pitcher

                refreshes th thirst of
ny memory, her limbs thrust
er fingers flying to my stroke

Under th mattress, a field of snow crystal
ry as th sun's heat
nakes th rainbow glow

eb./67

he canadian

  On the train, back from th Empress
lining car, snowing woodlands
pulling thru Manitoba, recall
  how sum yrs after th second centenary
f th founding of Halifax, which
  date i commemorated with sign
  above my father's street door,
nto two parts i divided, th half
n th left, what once was, before
749, th MicMac Indian, th second
alf, after that time, a British sailor,
n board, telescope to eye, sailing
  into harbor, Montbatten drove by
  my father's house that day, part of
h ceremonies, dressd by University gown
& cap, later that year, th woman to be
Queen, then Princess Elizabeth drove
  thru Halifax town, in bullet-proof car.

11   bill bissett

But i was to recall, as i did,
coming back from th dining car, that
sum yrs. after Halifax had her bicentenary,
i wrote my third or fourth pome, in
which, constructed as allegory, i did en
vision th society of fact in Canada
as a train, its peopuls classd, & sub-
classd, according to th rank & station,
that is, what they cud claim they owned,or,
who they cud claim owned them, its
peopuls cut off from each other by
        such coach cars & compartments.

And, i recall, part of th allegory, was
the train going thru th tunnel – darkness,
fortifying th condition,keeping each in place,
lest they overcome fear & th structure toppul.

It's not such a good allegory, my
friends sd – well, now that sum of my best
friends are in jail – i see its uses,
  my boyhood despair – seeing, as th
    train rolls thru Manitoba, how it
does seem that still peopul are hungry in
this country, sum of my best friends are
  hungry, peopul are hungry, they hunger
for food – outside of this train there is
  no food – in it there is good & bad food;
    food that will just keep yu strong enuff
      to keep yr place – food that is
      just good enuff yu dream
        of better food – and food that is so good
        yu become encouraged to accept
          that this train is not going to crash
          cannot be changed, from within
          or without, is God or Allah's very
          handiwork, but where is th food
          on this train, this one
            to show me Allah in all things,
          for then, in ourselves th best food,
            we share th bounty
              on this Iron Horse.

feb. 10/67

circles in th sun

In th mushroom village
all th littul children
brightly smiling

in th mushroom village
all th littul children
brightly be

asking only for th river
asking only for th river

dream for th snowfields
dream for th reindeer

living for th changes of gold and flesh
living for th changes of gold and flesh

its got hair on it moves west is only blessd
its got hair on it moves west is only blessd

what it smells like th burning fire
of yr soul tunnels thru th mountains
like meat like yolk
as precious thots
birthd by th union
of th lightning
flashes that blind
yr will

and th children sleep
soft till dawn all
around them th jackal creep

o love past play past memory
let th children be
let th children be

113   bill bissett

ode to frank silvera

yu might think that moving
silently thru th tenement
yr holsters bright nd lively
in th yellow colord air

yu might think that yr horse
kickin without sound at th moon
where sum say th faild souls
those who cant find bodies hang
out

yu might say movin soft on top
of egg shell tord yr path, karma
is will plus fate, th old time
blend

yu might hope there is sum one
to love yu at th end of th road
yu might see nothin can grow in
th dust of yr anxieties

yu might say that fate is whats left
aftr yu do nothing. yu can go on
alone with all th mysteries of being.

yu walk out of th town at sun rise
before there is sound th fields
maybe yu get rheumatism from too
much mornin dew maybe yr hungr gets
too deep to drink maybe yr holsters
get parchd maybe theres only silence

yu might say there is always
more love of dark and golden being

yu might say yul fly
more like th crow

yu cud say yu dont have to kill
yrself that'l be taken care of

yu cud say th mountain and love is
hard and eternal. never yields to
nothing. sumtime yu are th wind
racing green ovr th hairy fields

sumtimes yu are th blind eye
of th sun turning in yr belly

yu dream

yu move further out a town

my friends give me back feeling

maybe sumwhun will cum nd take us
away rescue us gathr us up together
all how ever many we are into covrd
wagons take us to where sumwhere
weve never herd of before deep
in th glowing woods she held my hand

Gwendolyn MacEwen

The Kindled Children

in summer you invoked a fire for children –
you aimed a small lens at the sun and kindled a twig
beneath it. You had that much time to do it –
that much of a magnified afternoon for the children's kindling.

now this innocence confounds me, this ability to stand
hours beneath the prolonged sun, expanding light
in the exploding novum of their eyes, and
without anger at the world's turn, its argument into night.

impossible to know where your anger lies!
in my burning world I must protract time
down to the worlds of my fevered hands
holding knives to carve the lithic minutes of my lines.

and in the kindling unquiet of my brain I recall
all kinds of burning times – a night in fall
when suns went silently nova, light years beyond
your unlit room, and other times, but always the burning

ensues upon my watching you, in summer and in other seasons
when you do not argue the day into night, as I do,
when you hook a whole afternoon into a small lens
and change it into fire for the kindled children,
when you move about, having little need
of wider fires, whole burning worlds, or anything
beyond the intact moments of your deeds.

The Children Are Laughing

It is monday and the children are laughing
The children are laughing; they believe they are princes
They wear no shoes; they believe they are princes
And their filthy kingdom heaves up behind them

The filthy city heaves up behind them
They are older than I am, their feet are shoeless
They have lived a thousand years; the children are laughing
The children are laughing and their death is upon them

I have cried in the city (the children are laughing)
I have worn many colours (the children are laughing)
They are older than I am, their death is upon them
I will wear no shoes when the princes are dying

For Hart Crane

the images, the images removed ten times
and taut as cables straddling
gaps of strange tension, find finally
reality crutched in the Bridge's armpits
or in the charged spaces between breaths –

the sun, tho, pinpoint and tidy on sundays
is no consolation; the combless hair of waves
erases vision; ferneries fumble
clarity; you alone have watched steel crumble.

now I speak of you as your own kingdom
ruling an empire of conglomerate provinces
from an undersea,

as, sick of focus
on a blind skyline, a crashed circumference,
your neck was free to bend from that swaying deck
down, down to the crazy heaven of the fishes.

The Last Breakfast

sometimes the food refuses to be sanctified
and you stand over the table beating your chest
and screaming impotent graces for bacon and eggs
graphic on the plate, arranged in a greasy cipher

aware that your body like a graceful vegetable
refuses to be holy, you stop screaming
grace for the eggs and the unsacred bacon,
you stop screaming and sit down darkly

hypnotized by two fried yellow eggs, by this
altogether kanadian breakfast, realizing
your appetite is jaded and the plate is blue
and the food has become an anathema

the bacon has nothing to say for itself
the whole thing is decidedly insane
but you eat the breakfast because it is there
to be eaten, and as you eat
you delicate barbarian, you think of pigs and chickens,
you think of mammoths and their tons of frozen ancient meat.
you think of dark men running through the earth
on their naked, splendid feet

The Magician

(for Raymond Lowe)

finally then the hands must play mad parables
finally then, the fingers' genius
wave out what my poems have said;
finally then must the silks occur
                                    plus rabbits
and the big umbrellas be
spun on stage continually.

as you Lowe, in quiet irony
inspire terrible skills of silks
                      or crash scarves vertically
as though miniature brains were held in fingertips
fantastic as of secrecy –

or my art being more a lie anyway
than the lie of these illusions
secreting realities in the twitching silks
or sacred sleeves
                  to twist or tamper them
to come out solid, in cubes or cups –
pull down then
              silk avalanche of scarves
or play the cosmos on strings of human hair
                      as a wand cracks
and blinds belief and holds it knotted
          like an ugly necklace
          or a hopeless rope –

or you, Lowe, driving a spike through the head of a boy
as though magic were (and is)
a nail of steel to split the skull

in either direction
to believe or not believe
is not the question.

finally then do all my poems become as crazy scarves
issuing from the fingers in a coloured mesh
and you magician, stand as they fly around you
silent as Houdini who could escape from anything
except the prison of his own flesh.

Manzini: Escape Artist

now there are no bonds except the flesh; listen –
there was this boy, Manzini, stubborn with
gut stood with black tights and a turquoise
leaf across his sex

and smirking while the big
brute tied his neck arms legs, Manzini
naked waist up and white with sweat

struggled. Silent, delinquent, he
was suddenly all teeth and knee, straining slack
and excellent with sweat, inwardly

wondering if Houdini would take as long
as he; fighting time and the drenched
muscular ropes, as though his tendons were worn
on the outside –

as though his own guts were the ropes
encircling him; it was beautiful; it was thursday; listen –
there was this boy, Manzini

finally free, slid as snake from
his own sweet agonized skin, to throw his entrails
white upon the floor
with a cry of victory –

now there are no bonds except the flesh,
but listen, it was thursday, there was this boy,
Manzini –

The Garden of Square Roots: An Autobiography

and then the rattlesnake spines of men distracted me
for even they, the people were
as Natajara was, who danced
while I was anchored like a passive verb
or Neptune on a subway –

and from the incredible animal i
grew queer claws inward to fierce cribs;
I searched gardens for square roots,
for i was the I interior
the thing with a gold belt and delicate ears
with no knees or elbows
was working from the inside out

this city I live in I built with bones
and mortared with marrow;
I planned it in my spare time
and its hydro is charged from a blood niagara
and I built this city backwards and
the people evolved out of the buildings
and the subway uterus ejected them –

for i was the I interior
the thing with a gold belt and delicate ears
with no knees or elbows
was working from the inside out.

and all my gardens grew backwards
and all the roots were finally square
and Ah! the flowers grew there like algebra

The Red Bird You Wait For

You are waiting for someone to confirm it,
You are waiting for someone to say it plain,
Now we are here and because we are short of time
I will say it; I might even speak its name.

It is moving above me, it is burning my heart out,
I have felt it crash through my flesh,
I have spoken to it in a foreign tongue,
I have stroked its neck in the night like a wish.

Its name is the name you have buried in your blood,
Its shape is a gorgeous cast-off velvet cape,
Its eyes are the eyes of your most forbidden lover
And its claws, I tell you its claws are gloved in fire.

You are waiting to hear its name spoken,
You have asked me a thousand times to speak it,
You who have hidden it, cast if off, killed it,
Loved it to death and sung your songs over it.

The red bird you wait for falls with giant wings –
A velvet cape whose royal colour calls us kings
Is the form it takes as, uninvited, it descends,
It is the Power and the Glory forever, Amen.

The Discovery

do not imagine that the exploration
ends, that she has yielded all her mystery
or that the map you hold
cancels further discovery

I tell you her uncovering takes years,
takes centuries, and when you find her naked
look again,
admit there is something else you cannot name,
a veil, a coating just above the flesh
which you cannot remove by your mere wish

when you see the land naked, look again
(burn your maps, that is not what I mean),
I mean the moment when it seems most plain
is the moment when you must begin again

Inside the Great Pyramid

all day the narrow shaft
received us; everyone
came out sweating and
gasping for air, and one
old man collapsed
upon a stair;
                    I thought:

the fact that it has stood
so long
is no guarantee
it will stand today,
but went in anyway
and heard when I was
halfway up a long
low rumbling like
the echo of ancient stones
first straining to their place;
           I thought:
we have made this, we
have made *this*.
I scrambled out into
the scandalous sun and saw
the desert was an hourglass
we had forgotten to invert,
a tasselled camel falling
to his knees, the River
filling the great waterclock
of earth.

Cairo, 1966

Dark Pines Under Water

This land like a mirror turns you inward
And you become a forest in a furtive lake;
The dark pines of your mind reach downward,
You dream in the green of your time,
Your memory is a row of sinking pines.

Explorer, you tell yourself this is not what you came for
Although it is good here, and green;
You had meant to move with a kind of largeness,
You had planned a heavy grace, an anguished dream.

But the dark pines of your mind dip deeper
And you are sinking, sinking, sleeper
In an elementary world;
There is something down there and you want it told.

The Heel

In the organing dark I bless those who came from the
  waters
scaleless and shrewd, and walked with unwebbed feet
to create memory, when every movement invented their
  end,
who stood beside the holy waters with upright spines
to destroy themselves, to inherit themselves, to stand
while the fish fell back and the waves erased their birth.

They were terrible with sense and torn at the tongue
and in the foreign hours when fog enveloped them
they thrashed like swimmers down the rivers of their
  sleep;
the sunken cities within them rose and towered high
over the bright groin of their pain, and elsewhere
they were lovers and their knees were pyramids of fire.

I bless those who turned the double face of memory
  around,
who turned on their naked green heels and had great
  dreams
and in the queer hour when they are struck at the eyes
and the last sunrise claims and cripples them, I stand
and remark that on the edge of this strand I also feel
the holy waters lapping just behind my heel.

Michael Ondaatje

"Description is a Bird"

In the afternoon while the sun twists down
they come piggle piggle piggle all around the air.
Under clouds of horses the sand swallows turn

quick and gentle as wind.
All virtuoso performances
that presume a magnificent audience.

The leader flings his neck back,
turns thinner than whims.
Like God the others follow
anticipating each twist,
the betrayals of a feather.

For them no thumping wing beat of a crow,
they bounce on a breath
scattering with the discipline of a watch.

Dragon

I have been seeing dragons again.
Last night, hunched on a beaver dam,
one held a body like a badly held cocktail;
his tail, keeping the beat of a waltz,
sent a morse of ripples to my canoe.

They are not richly bright
but muted like dawns
or the vague sheen on a fly's wing.
Their old flesh drags in folds
as they drop into grey pools,
strain behind a tree.

Finally the others saw one today, trapped,
tangled in our badminton net.
The minute eyes shuddered deep in the creased face
while his throat, strangely fierce, stretched
to release an extinct burning inside:
pathetic loud whispers as four of us
and the excited spaniel surrounded him.

Signature

The car carried him
racing the obvious moon
beating in the trees like a white bird.

Difficult to make words sing
around your appendix.
The obvious upsets me,
everyone has scars which crawl
into the mystery of swimming trunks.

I was the first appendix in my family;
my brother who was given the stigma
of a rare blood type,
proved to have ulcers instead.

The rain fell like applause as I approached the hospital.

It takes seven seconds she said,
strapped my feet,
entered my arm.
I stretched all senses
on FIVE
the room closed on me like an eyelid.

At night the harmonica plays,
a whistler joins in respect.
I am a sweating marble saint
full of demerol and sleeping pills.
A man in the armour of shining plaster
walks to my door, then past.
Imagine the rain
falling like white bees on the sidewalk
imagine Snyder
high on poetry and mountains

Three floors down
my appendix
swims in a jar

O world, I shall be buried all over Ontario

Henri Rousseau and Friends

(for Bill Muysson)

In his clean vegetation
the parrot, judicious,
poses on a branch.
The narrator of the scene,
aware of the perfect fruits,
the white and blue flowers,
the snake with an ear for music;
he presides.

The apes
hold their oranges like skulls,
like chalices.
They are below the parrot
above the oranges –
a jungle serfdom which
with this order
reposes.

They are the ideals of dreams.
Among the exactness,
the symmetrical petals,
the efficiently flying angels,
there is complete liberation.
The parrot is interchangeable;
tomorrow in its place
a waltzing man and tiger,
brash legs of a bird.

Greatness achieved
they loll among textbook flowers

And in this pose hang
scattered like pearls
in just as intense a society.
On Miss Adelaide Milton de Groot's walls,
with Lillie P. Bliss in New York.

And there too
in spangled wrists and elbows
and grand facades of cocktails
are vulgarly beautiful parrots, appalled lions,
the beautiful and the forceful locked in suns,
and the slight, careful stepping birds.

27   Michael Ondaatje

As Thurber would say – C*ws

By 7:10 they have finally shuddered
the last of the night off
and can be regarded as awake.
But even awake they keep the presence
(coiling sleep)
of Italian restaurant owners.

And all the energy is in the tail of the cow.
It is their one pound of flesh
that lives up to the Twentieth Century,
the one troublesome cockerel in the barn
rising like a pyjama cord
to bring these bony animals to life.

My wife is the tail of the cow;
she coaxes me up in the morning
removing bedclothes and body
and throws a breakfast at me
demanding appreciative nods at 6 a.m.

But these animals
with the energy of their manure
are drifting summer
and all the seasons
ferment with ease in their udders.
Even their desires are supplied.

O for a professional poke
from a thick thighed
black pedigree.

"Lovely the Country of Peacocks"

My daughter cackling in defiance
voices mystic yells like a snake charmer,
a fulica in the afternoon.

Her buddhist stomach is boasted,
there is an interest in toes.
In rusty actions
she struggles for tender goals:

her mother's hair,
the crumpled paper.
Her retaliations to matches,
muscles, and hairy dogs
are all degreed.
Looking on
we wear sentimentality like a curse.

Her body bears, inside the changing flesh,
rivers of collected suns,
jungles of force, coloured birds
and laziness.

Pyramid

For days they had toiled
sun baked, naked,
raging in the sun
their yells muted in the vast afternoons.
In rhythm they swung like leaves
and broke the horizon
nails
joining the starched blue to sand.

And while it grew
I watched them heave
trailing their boulders to the moon
and at dusk saw the shadows run.

Timeless here
they perfected degrees
allowing for heat and burn
and to pulsed commands
jack-knifed lime chimes.
Those were their minutes,
distant I saw them mime pains
and saw their bodies churn,
pivot, sweat leaving them oiled.

And finishing they circled and prayed
and led me deep into the ground,
positioned me by a mirror
and sealed the form they made.

I watch
and in our conversations
grow profound.

The Goodnight

With the bleak heron Paris
imagine Philoctetes
the powerful fat thighed man,
the bandaged smelling foot
with rivers of bloodshot veins
scattering like trails into his thighs:
a man who roared on an island for ten years,
whose body grew banal
while he stayed humane
behind the black teeth and withering hair.

Imagine in his hands – black
from the dried blood of animals,
a bow of torn silver
that noised arrows loose like a wild heart;

in front of him – Paris
darting and turning, the perfumed stag,
and beyond him the sun
netted in the hills, throwing back his shape,
until the running spider of shadow
gaped on the bandaged foot of the standing man
who let shafts of eagles into the ribs
that were moving to mountains.

Paris

(Part II)

We would visit the city
lined like the old man's face,
see King Priam at the games
striding in his age and state,
the eyes strange, the walk unnecessarily heavy,
the prudish Hector awing him,
and when angered
calmed only by the young Polyxena.

In games standing knee locked
I drove, and with a flourish
tilted chariot to chants.
And seeing Oinone's eyes
proud and wild
among my tears of speed,
hunched my body into a gracious bow
and left the chariot in a vast
ignoble, timeless tumble.

Then her gentle body
frail in the mornings
and white in the streams
gleaming among the dark rocks of Ida
while dawns grew over the hill.
Those days we sprawled on banks
or toed dust in silence.

"For Alexandros who understands."
"Who understands what?"
"Everything."

These Are the Killed

These Are the Killed

(By me) –
Morton, Baker, early friends of mine.
Joe Bernstein. 3 Indians.
A blacksmith when I was twelve, with a knife.
5 Indians in self defence (behind a very safe rock).
One man who bit me during a robbery.
Brady, Hindman, Beckwith, Joe Clark,
Deputy Jim Carlyle, Deputy Sheriff J. W. Bell.
And Bob Ollinger. A rabid cat
birds during practice,

These are the killed.

(By them) –
Charlie, Tom O'Folliard
Angela D's split arm,
                and Pat Garrett
sliced off my head.
Blood a necklace on me all my life.

In Boot Hill

In Boot Hill there are over 400 graves. It takes
the space of 7 acres. There is an elaborate gate
but the path keeps to no main route for it tangles
like branches of a tree among the gravestones.

300 of the dead in Boot Hill died violently
200 by guns, over 50 by knives
some were pushed under trains – a popular
and overlooked form of murder in the west.
Some from brain haemorrhages resulting from bar fights
at least 10 killed in barbed wire.

In Boot Hill there are only two graves that belong to women
and they are the only known suicides in that graveyard

Gregory

After shooting Gregory
this is what happened

I'd shot him well and careful
made it explode under his heart
so it wouldnt last long and
was about to walk away
when this chicken paddles out to him
and as he was falling hops on his neck
digs the beak into his throat
straightens legs and heaves
a red and blue vein out

Meanwhile he fell
and the chicken walked away

still tugging at the vein
till it was 12 yards long
as if it held that body like a kite
Gregory's last words being

get away from me yer stupid chicken

Pat Garrett

Pat Garrett, ideal assassin. Public figure, the mind of a doctor, his
hands hairy, scarred, burned by rope, on his wrist there was a purple
stain there all his life. Ideal assassin for his mind was unwarped. Had
the ability to kill someone on the street walk back and finish a joke.
One who had decided what was right and forgot all morals. He was
genial to everyone even his enemies. He genuinely enjoyed people,
some who were odd, the dopes, the thieves. Most dangerous for
them, he understood them, what motivated their laughter and anger,
what they liked to think about, how he had to act for them to like
him. An academic murderer – only his vivacious humour and diverse
interests made him the best kind of company. He would listen to
people like Rudabaugh and giggle at their escapades. His language
was atrocious in public, yet when alone he never swore.

At the age of 15 he taught himself French and never told anyone about it and never spoke to anyone in French for the next 40 years. He didnt even read French books.

Between the ages of 15 and 18 little was heard of Garrett. In Juan Para he bought himself a hotel room for two years with money he had saved and organised a schedule to learn how to drink. In the first three months he forced himself to disintegrate his mind. He would vomit everywhere. In a year he could drink two bottles a day and not vomit. He began to dream for the first time in his life. He would wake up in the mornings, his sheets soaked in urine 40% alcohol. He became frightened of flowers because they grew so slowly that he couldn't tell what they planned to do. His mind learned to be superior because of the excessive mistakes of those around him. Flowers watched him.

After two years he could drink anything mix anything together and stay awake and react just as effectively as when sober. But he was now addicted, locked in his own game. His money was running out. He had planned the drunk to last only two years, now it continued into new months over which he had no control. He stole and sold himself to survive. One day he was robbing the house of Juanita Martinez, was discovered by her, and collapsed in her living room. In about six months she had un-iced his addiction. They married and two weeks later she died of a consumption she had hidden from him.

What happened in Garrett's mind no one knows. He did not drink, was never seen. A month after Juanita Garrett's death he arrived in Sumner.

PAULITA MAXWELL:

> I remember the first day Pat Garrett ever set foot in Fort Sumner. I was a small girl with dresses at my shoe-tops and when he came to our house and asked for a job, I stood behind my brother Pete and stared at him in open eyed wonder; he had the longest legs I'd ever seen and he looked so comical and had such a droll way of talking that after he was gone, Pete and I had a good laugh about him.

His mind was clear, his body able to drink, his feelings, unlike those who usually work their own way out of hell, not cynical about another's incapacity to get out of problems and difficulties. He did ten years of ranching, cow punching, being a buffalo hunter. He married Apolinaria Guitterrez and had five sons. He had come to Sumner then, mind full of French he never used, everything equipped to be that rare thing – a sane assassin sane assassin sane assassin sane assassin sane assassin sane

Poor Young William's Dead

Poor young William's dead
with a fish stare, with a giggle
with blood planets in his head.

The blood came down like river tide
long as Texas down his side.
We cleaned him up when blood was drier
his eyes looked up like turf on fire.

We got the eight foot garden hose
turned it on, leaned him down flat.
What fell away we threw away
his head was smaller than a rat.

I got the bullets, cleaned him up
sold them to the Texas Star.
They weighed them, put them in a pile
took pictures with a camera.

Poor young William's dead
with blood planets in his head
with a fish stare, with a giggle
like he said.

Bibliographical Notes

AL PURDY (born 1918) published *The Enchanted Echo* (1944), *Pressed on sand* (1955), *Emu remember!* (1957) *The Crafte So Long to Lerne* (1959), *Poems for All the Annettes* (1962), and *The Blur in Between* (1963). A revised edition of *Poems for All the Annettes* (1968), with additional selections from the earlier books, "amounts to a 'Selected Poems' – prior to 1965"; for *Cariboo Horses* (1965) Purdy received the Governor-General's Award. He has since published *North of Summer* (1967), *Wild Grape Wine* (1968), *Love in a Burning Building* (1970), and has edited two important anthologies, *Fifteen Winds* (1969), and *Storm Warning* (1971). Writer, editor, critic, former vagrant and factory worker, Purdy has held several Canada Council Fellowships.

MILTON ACORN (born 1923). His publications include *In Love and Anger* (1956), *Against a League of Liars* (1960), *The Brain's the Target* (1960), *Jawbreakers* (1963), and *I've Tasted My Blood*, a selection of poems from 1956 to 1968, edited by Al Purdy. For this selection, Acorn was honoured by poets across Canada who presented him with an award created for the occasion. In 1963 *Fiddlehead* devoted a special edition to Acorn's poems, *58 poems by Milton Acorn*. He describes himself as a revolutionary poet and a thousandth generation Canadian. Senior Award Winner of Canada Council.

JOE ROSENBLATT (born 1933). The author of two books of poetry: *The LSD Leacock* (1966) and *Winter of the Luna Moth* (1968); associated with a variety of poetic endeavours, from the free speech movement at Allan Gardens to *Jewish Dialogue*, Rosenblatt is presently completing a third book, *Bumblebee Mantras*. He holds awards from the Canada Council and the Ontario Arts Council. A former welder, plumber, and railway worker, he now writes and draws.

LEONARD COHEN (born 1934). Published five books of poetry, two novels, a collection of his songs, and produced three records of his songs. His books of poetry include *Let Us Compare Mythologies* (1956); *The Spice-Box of Earth* (1961); *Flowers for Hitler* (1964); and *Parasites of Heaven* (1966). His *Selected Poems: 1956 – 1968* won the Governor-General's Award though Cohen found himself unable to accept the honour. His two novels are *The Favourite Game* (1963) and *Beautiful Losers* (1966). Aside from the record albums, his songs appear as *Songs of Leonard Cohen*. A wandering singer, he confines himself to occasional appearances on concert circuit and to recordings.

GEORGE BOWERING (born 1935). Books of poems include *Sticks and Stones* (1963), *Points on the Grid* (1964), *The Man in Yellow Boots* (1965), *The Silver Wire* (1966), *Baseball* (1967), *Two Police Poems* (1968); he received the Governor-General's Award in 1969 for two books of poetry, *Rocky Mountain Foot*, and *The Gangs of Kosmos*. His novel, *Mirror on the Floor*, was published in 1967. Bowering is a Professor of English at Sir George Williams University.

JOHN NEWLOVE (born 1938). Publications include *Grave Sirs* (1962), *Elephants, Mothers & Others* (1963), *Moving in Alone* (1965), *Notebook Pages* (1966), *What They Say* (1967), *Black Night Window* (1968), *The Cave* (1970) and *7 Disasters, 3 Theses, and Welcome Home. Click* (1971). Mr. Newlove, now senior editor in a publishing house, has received several Canada Council Awards.

MARGARET ATWOOD (born 1939). For her first book of poems *The Circle Game* (1966), she received the Governor-General's Award. Other books of poetry include *The Animals in That Country* (1968), *The Journals of Susanna Moodie* (1970), *Procedures for underground* (1970), and *Power Politics* (1971). Her novel, *The Edible Woman*, appeared in 1969. Winner of a Senior Canada Council Award, Miss Atwood has taught at Sir George Williams University, University of British Columbia, University of Alberta at Edmonton, and York University.

BILL BISSETT (born 1939). His poetry is published by small presses and in limited editions including *We sleep inside each other all* (1966), *Fires in th Tempul* (1967), *What poetiks* (1967), *Lebanon Voices* (1967), *Gossamer Bedpan* (1968), *Th Table Moves, Sunday Work* (1968), *Lost Angel Mining Company* (1969), *Liberating Skies, Th Outlaw* (1970) and *Awake in th red desert: a recorded book* (1968). His poems can also be found in *West Coast Seen* (1969), an anthology of West Coast Writers, and in Purdy's *Storm Warning* (1971), an anthology of young writers. Bissett has held several Canada Council Awards. He is an artist, painter, poet, and full-time visionary.

GWENDOLYN MACEWEN (born 1941). She has published three books of poetry and a novel. The novel, entitled *Julian the Magician*, appeared in 1963. Her books of poetry include *The Rising Fire* (1963), *A Breakfast for Barbarians* (1966); and *The Shadow-Maker* (1969) for which she received the Governor-General's Award. She has been awarded a Canada Council Fellowship and is presently completing a second novel.

MICHAEL ONDAATJE (born 1943). His publications include three books of poetry, *The Dainty Monsters* (1967), *The Man with Seven Toes* (1969), and *The Collected Works of Billy the Kid* (1970) which received the Governor-General's Award. He has also published a critical study, *Leonard Cohen* (1970) and has produced a film, *Sons of Captain Poetry*, featuring b. p. Nichol. He also edited *The Broken Ark*, an anthology of animal poems (1971). Ondaatje is now Assistant Professor of English at Glendon College, York University.

Acknowledgements

This page constitutes an extension of the copyright page. We wish to thank the following authors, publishers, and copyright holders for their kind permission to reproduce the poems in this book.

MILTON ACORN: for selections from *I've Tasted My Blood*. For personal and public reasons, Mr. Acorn has declared all poems in the above volume in the public domain.

HOUSE OF ANANSI PRESS: for selections from *The Collected Works of Billy the Kid* by Michael Ondaatje; for "Thru," "Particulars on the Picture Cards," "The Envies" and "On Quadra Island," from *Gangs of Kosmos* by George Bowering; for "Uncle Nathan," "A Salmon Dying," "The Painted Bird," "The Butterfly Bat," "The Electric Rose," "The Black Flower," "Marian," "Better She Dressed in a Black Garment" and "Sun Poem" from *Winter of the Luna Moth* by Joe Rosenblatt; for "This is a Photograph of Me," "After the Flood, We," "On the Streets, Love," "Journey to the Interior" and "A Place: Fragments," from *The Circle Game* by Margaret Atwood; for "They Eat Out" from *Power Politics* by Margaret Atwood; for WE SLEEP INSIDE EACH OTHER ALL, from *We sleep inside each other all* by bill bissett; for "water eyes," "our moon," "lost yr way," "song composed just after th alarm clock before going to social assistance," "heat makes th heart's window" and "th canadian" from *awake in th red desert* by bill bissett; for "circles in th sun," "my friends give me back feeling" and "ode to frank silvera" from *lost angel mining company* by bill bissett.

THE MACMILLAN COMPANY OF CANADA LIMITED: for "The Red Bird You Wait For," "The Discovery," "Inside the Great Pyramid," "Dark Pines Under Water" and "The Heel" from *The Shadow-Maker* by Gwendolyn MacEwen.

MCCLELLAND AND STEWART LIMITED: for "The Blue," "Indian Summer," "Footprints, Fenceposts" and "Forget" from *Rocky Mountain Foot* by George Bowering; for the selections from *Selected Poems* by Leonard Cohen; for selections from *Black Night Window* by John Newlove; for "Necropsy of Love," "Mountain Lions in Stanley Park," "Mice in the House," "Home-Made Beer," "The Country North of Belleville" and "To An Attempted Suicide" from *Cariboo Horses* by Al Purdy; for "Trees at the Arctic Circle" and "Innuit" from *North of Summer* by Al Purdy; for "Elegy for a Grandfather,"

"Detail," "Interruption," "Wilderness Gothic," "Lament for the
Dorsets," "Beothuk Indian Skeleton in a Glass Case" and
"Remains of an Indian Village" from *Wild Grape Wine* by
Al Purdy. Reprinted by permission of The Canadian Publishers,
McClelland and Stewart Limited, Toronto.

THE RYERSON PRESS, MCGRAW-HILL COMPANY OF CANADA
LIMITED: for selections from *Breakfast for Barbarians* by
Gwendolyn MacEwen, by permission of The McGraw-Hill
Company of Canada Limited, Toronto.

MICHAEL ONDAATJE: for "Description is a Bird," "Dragon,"
"Signature," "Henri Rousseau and Friends," "As Thurber would
say – C*ws," "Lovely the Country of Peacocks," "Pyramid,"
"The Goodnight" and "Paris (Part II)" from *The Dainty
Monsters*. Coach House Press, Toronto, 1967. Copyright Michael
Ondaatje. Reprinted by permission of the author.

AL PURDY: for "After the Rats," "Gilgamesh and Friend,"
"The Listeners" and "On the Decipherment of 'Linear B'," from
Poems for All the Annettes. House of Anansi, 1968. Reprinted
by permission of the author.

OXFORD UNIVERSITY PRESS: for "The animals in that country,"
"The Landlady," "At the tourist centre in Boston," "A night in
the Royal Ontario Museum," "The gods avoid revealing
themselves" and "Backdrop addresses cowboy" from *The
Animals in That Country* by Margaret Atwood; for "Girl and
Horse, 1928," "Procedures for Underground" and "Younger
Sister, Going Swimming," from *Procedures for Underground* by
Margaret Atwood; for "Further Arrivals" and "Departure from
the Bush" from *The Journals of Sussana Moodie* by Margaret
Atwood.

JOHN NEWLOVE: for "Everywhere I Go" from *7 Disasters, 3
Theses, and Welcome Home. Click*. Reprinted by permission of
the author.

JOE ROSENBLATT: for "Breakfast I," "Breakfast II," "The Easter
Egg I Got for Passover," "The Mole," Jealousy," "Heliotrope"
and "Metamorpho I," from *The LSD Leacock*. Coach House
Press, Toronto, 1966. Reprinted by permission of the author.